Reboot Your Reputation

Elva R Ainsworth

Edited by Julie Lewthwaite

Cover design and chapter graphic by Sean Strong

Dedication

*To anyone who has been upset
by feedback - this is for you!*

Acknowledgements

Thank you to everyone in the Talent Innovations team for their tireless work and support in this area. It is only because you are all getting on with business so well that I get the chance to write. This book would not be written without all your help.

Thank you.

Contents

About the author

Elva Ainsworth was born into a family of people-watchers and has cultivated a real love of people pattern spotting. This combination led her to a career in HR after a psychology degree at Bristol University. In HR she enjoyed implementing the brand new psychometrics, as well as designing culture change and personal development tools.

In 1994 she focused on her love of psychometrics by joining SHL (now CEB), the leading business psychologists, where she managed the 360° feedback and management development practice in both the UK and in the USA. Qualifying in homeopathy was combined with her OD perspective to feed a strong appetite for a new approach to giving feedback. Elva has published her first book, "*360 Degree Feedback: A Transformational Approach*", available on Amazon.

360 DEGREE FEEDBACK:
A Transformational Approach

Introducing Talent Innovations

Founded in 2002 by Elva Ainsworth, a leading authority on the subject of 360° feedback, Talent Innovations is a boutique consultancy specialising in the planning and delivery of 360° and continual feedback programmes. Talent Innovations' expertise in this area is substantiated by extensive experience in the fields of HR, psychometrics, 360° feedback coaching, data analysis and transformational development.

Talent Innovations attracts organisations that require a programme that can be moulded to their culture, engages individuals, and provides strikingly clear insights from the feedback process.

Talent Innovations offers a secure online platform for sophisticated and customisable 360° and continuous feedback projects, with strong psychometric features. It has been meticulously developed to provide users with easy-to-use software that encourages personalis-ation, giving individuals real ownership of their feedback and control of the process.

Talent Innovations has formulated transformational partnerships with Transport for London, Jaguar Land Rover, Virgin, Tate, Christie's, University of York and the General Medical Council. The portfolio includes the development of strategic competency frameworks, 360° feedback and performance management tools, data-driven coaching and leadership development tools, and consultancy.

See www.talentinnovations.com for further details.

Preface

This book is written for anyone upset or frustrated with what other people think about them. You may have just received some feedback via a 360° feedback process or simply by hearing or sensing what people think. You may be feeling mortified or confused, resigned or disappointed, angry or even outraged. In my work with senior leaders I have seen all of this and felt just a glimpse of their pain. It is still hard to observe and clearly difficult to bear. Some of these opinions are deeply disempowering and are not easy to turn around. In fact some of them, especially those founded on inherited stereotypic influences, are way beyond the power of any one individual to challenge, never mind change.

When you are committed to a particular goal where opinions work against you, you will experience this negative force on a daily and moment-to-moment basis. Rather than give up or take the failure as a personal result, this book takes you on a journey through to understanding these opinions as fluid and dynamic, and being in your control. Once you can see you have a level of control you will then be able to "reboot" your reputation by choosing between the eleven practical ways described to find a way forward that empowers you. It is time to drop the anger and the powerlessness, let the disappointment go and pick up something that will help you progress.

Introduction

What other people think of you should not matter, but it does. Some of us spend years working out how to have it not matter, others pretend they do not care, while the rest have not noticed that it does. But it really makes a difference, regardless of your point of view. Others' opinions can make us feel good or bad. They can bolster or diminish. But something more critical happens. Even neutrality and "nothingness" can have the consequence of diminishing you in a context where support is expected or needed. Others' opinions can either make you bigger or they can make it harder for you.

Your ability and potential to act and be a leader, at work and in life in general, is dependent on others agreeing to work with you. Your effectiveness depends on their eagerness to follow you and engage with you. Their view of you directly impacts how they listen to you; i.e., they will listen to what you say, and do so through the filters of their opinions. The extreme positions illustrate this. A leader you highly respect will be heard and you will likely regard their suggestions with openness and trust. You may then do what they ask you, if you can. A leader you do not respect will likely be avoided, challenged or ignored. Your view of them will therefore impact their ability to deliver and their experience of the relationship. It matters.

In over twenty years of working with at least 1,000 x 360° feedback reports, I noticed how useful it was for people to see what others see of them. The insight may be painful to process but in the end it is really useful to know - much more useful than not knowing. However, knowing what other people think is just the beginning of a transformational journey. Once you have got to a position of understanding and accepting the data, you may then be left with the question of, "*I get that they have these opinions about me, but what am I supposed to do about it?*" In seeing the opinions you may also get clear on the impact and consequences of such opinions, but you may still be left with uncertainty as to what you can do. Some things you might be able to fix, but even fixing yourself does not guarantee that anyone will notice! My experience with very senior female executives and non-white male leaders showed up another problem: people's views are not always specific and personal to you. Instead they can be stereotypic and prejudicial in nature. Hard to spot, but these views are bigger than you and represent a bias outside of any one individual's control. And, worse than this, you may not even notice it's going on.

So views may be impacting you negatively and you have no control. Time to get upset, cross and give up? No; here are eleven strategies to improve and manage your situation. Try them. Enjoy them, and let's work together for a future where conscious evaluation trumps prejudice every time.

CHAPTER 1

Feedback is always specific to you,
but never personal

You have just had some feedback, a clear glimpse of how others are seeing you. You are reeling a little from this information. You are not sure what to think or quite how best to deal with this. If that is where you are right now, this book is for you. Take your time to process the feedback and read through the book at a pace that matches your speed of processing. It has been written to hold your hand through a journey from insight to action, translating new data to a new you. You will see that even though there are plenty of things you can do to change things, you do not necessarily need to fix yourself or patch up your faults. In fact, you do not need to do anything unless you choose to.

The key thing to see is that it is you, and only you, who caused these opinions you have just seen, and as a result this means that these opinions are in your hands. No one else's. It is your reputation and it is your call. This book should help you feel better about your feedback and should allow you to see what your choices are.

Your feedback may have been given informally. You may have simply asked what someone thought or you may have been "told" without asking. You may have expected this feedback, maybe you have heard this before, or maybe not. It could be a total surprise. You may have gone through a formal process - perhaps a performance appraisal, received observations while you were on a training course, completed a selection exercise or you may have just gone through a full 360° feedback process; i.e., getting detailed data from all around you in the organisation (usually including your boss(es)), your direct reports/subordinates, peers/colleagues, your customers and internal/external stakeholders, and occasionally family). With all of these different methods of feedback there are a range of agendas going on.

The 360° experience is designed to explicitly encourage 8-20 people to say more than they might usually say. 360° is usually based on a detailed number of specific behaviours and typically encourages people to qualify their ratings and draft open text comments about you. Your reviewers are basically encouraged to say more of what they think than it is "normal" and OK to say. This can often bring fresh insights to light and can very easily cause you to feel overwhelmed with opinions that you may (quite rightfully!) feel are theirs, not yours. Given the resulting harshness of the 360° experience, the journey in this book will be tailored for this extreme position on the assumption that other examples will be covered also. So, wherever your tricky feedback has come from, the invitation is to put the feedback you have had firmly in one place with the assurance that you will be supported through a journey of processing. However you feel now, you will be OK by the end and you will have a number of strategies available for you to choose from, to manage and embrace your personal stereotype so it empowers you moving forward.

There is a recognised response to bad news - this can be seen illustrated in the **Elisabeth Kűbler-Ross** change curve (below) which she noticed when researching people who got news of a family member's life-limiting illness. There is an initial reaction, which is worth acknowledging as it can be very emotional and quite extreme.

Elisabeth Kűbler-Ross Change Curve

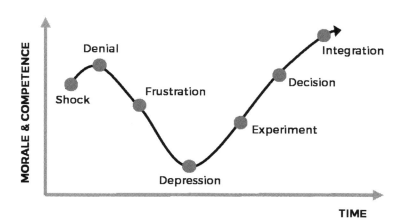

You can be shocked, in denial, and not wanting to look at it or think about it. You might then experience anger, frustration, desperation and depression as you start to process this information you really do not like. You may then start to get used to the idea, work out what you might do, start to understand how it is this way, and even be happy to talk about it. All of this is useful! The goal is for you to work this through until your self-esteem and self-image are at a higher place than when you started.

You will have grown as a result of this experience and will end up a bigger person. You will have overcome it, have an updated self-image that includes this data and is still OK. This is the goal and this is the purpose of this book - to support you through your emotional and intellectual journey to a more mature position of insight and self-awareness.

You may be surprised at the extent of your reactions. Current neuroscience gives us clues about why we might react like this. **David Rock** describes the "SCARF"[1] needs that people have in relation to feedback:

S	STATUS	Privacy is key here to ensuring humiliation is not overly public.
C	CERTAINTY	People really knowing what is happening with the data, who owns it, who will see it, etc., and knowing what the next steps are.
A	AUTONOMY	People need to feel in control of their destiny (even though in many respects they may not be!).
R	RELATEDNESS	People fear the data will impact their relationships, so reassurance and a sense that everything is OK helps.
F	FAIRNESS	People like to know the process and that other people are being fair, so reassurance of consistency of process may be useful.

With these needs you may be feeling that your reviewers have been unfair, that there has been something inconsistent or unexpected about the feedback process. You might feel a degree of outrage or irritation. If you are uncertain about how your data is to be shared or if you are thinking your feedback means your relationships and your job is at risk then you may be anxious about what this means. If you had not genuinely wanted this feedback, you may feel that you have been forced to participate in this process. This can feel like you have no control, which could be disarming for you. You may feel all these things! Regardless of these facts and how you might feel, please be reassured that you can regain control and security by working through some key points. You may need to give some things up and may need to be willing to shift your perspective on yourself and what is possible, but if you are open to developing a new strategy for yourself, then one is available.

Everybody can be susceptible and sensitive to feedback, but there are some types who are particularly vulnerable. First, if you see yourself as a perfectionist you are well set up to fail with any thorough detailed feedback mechanism. Such processes are designed to tell you what people want you to work on, what your weakest areas are, regardless of how good you are. The truth is that no one can be brilliant at absolutely everything. Why? Because "everything" includes many things that are antagonistic to others, and that simply do not co-exist simultaneously. An example of this is organisation skills, where our behavioural data demonstrates clearly that highly structured people are not highly flexible and open to impulse and change. A full list of these characteristics can be seen in my book on $360°^2$. It is simply impossible to be both structured and non-structured simultaneously, yet both styles have their value and place. Aiming for an impossible ideal of "perfection" may be core to your personality, but it can severely limit development and growth.

The second sensitive type to explore is the conscientious. If you are keen to get everything complete, to make sure you deliver everything on time, then your data may show up areas you have not completed that you were not aware about. You may feel mortified at such an idea, but please be assured that you are only human amongst other unreasonable humans and, in general, other people are bound to expect different things than they actually tell you. This means it is inevitable that there will be some areas of disappoint-ment. You are still OK and you can put things right.

The third type that might apply to you is the desire to be liked. If this is you, you are the popular one and that is how you get things done. Data showing up that you are not liked or even showing that some relationships are not as positive as you imagined will upset you greatly if this is the case. A glimpse of aspects "not liked" may upset you to the core, but some lower ratings and a challenging relationship does not necessarily mean it is the end of the world. A key stage in growth and development is to let go of the need to be liked[3]. This can be a painful thing to do in my personal experience, but definitely worth it as, once done, you will have many more choices available to you in terms of how to fulfil your commitments and you will have access to being OK when there is a breakdown in relationship with someone you care about. Do not worry, you will still be popular where it matters.

The fourth place where sensitivity can emerge is when those who have given you feedback are very important to you and you have not previously heard their voices. It may be a fresh relationship or maybe there has not been fully open and honest communication. This can often happen when there are big differences in seniority and/or confidence, which can lead one party to feel they cannot or should not express their opinions, and it can also happen when someone is keener to be positive and liked than they are to be fully honest. Given our British culture of seeming politeness, many 360° feedback situations throw up this example to a greater or lesser extent. Discovering that somebody has held a negative opinion about you but has not said anything or given any explicit clues can feel anything from slightly surprising to totally galling. It can feel as if you have been betrayed or tricked, and can leave you totally disempowered if you do not work it through. But the opportunity is offered to look at what exactly you did or said that had them think this, and then what caused you to not hear it. Then you are likely to see that the clues were there all the time...

If you are preparing to receive your feedback, it is worth noticing that you are likely to have some emotions and thoughts to deal with. This is because you, like others, are human and you care about what people think. Before you look at the feedback you are advised to prepare yourself. Taking a quick look as soon as you get the emailed report is one way, but you could alternatively set yourself up with a strategy to handle it well. There are some key things to consider:

First, be clear that you have a choice about whether you are open to accepting the feedback. It has been given to you, just like a Christmas gift you may get, and you can choose how to relate to it - just like you can choose how to relate to an unwanted present. Your choices are these:

* **Pretend it is fine, but not really pay it much attention; file it quickly**
* **Not even open it; leave it in your inbox unwrapped**
* **Decide it will be useless and throw it away**
* **Have a look and try it on; it might be really useful**
* **Be grateful and eager to understand, so you get the most from it**

Any of these are perfectly valid: you can choose. If you are not ready for feedback at any time then trust that you do know what you can handle and that you are doing the best thing for yourself. If you have got a lot of change and emotional trauma going on at the moment, for instance, dealing with work feedback could be the last thing you want, or should be facing.

If you have decided you want to look at your feedback then there are some golden rules to follow:

- **Pick your time and place carefully**

  Ensure you have some energy and space to read and review. You may want privacy or you may want to be home with your family.

- **Avoid things that might hinder mature processing, e.g. alcohol**

  It will not help you work it through calmly.

- **Ensure you have time to process**

  If you have a planned coaching or feedback session, then you will be in best shape to discuss it properly if you have had at least "two sleeps". Sleeping on it and having forty-eight hours of space seems to make a big difference. Your brain needs time to work things through and your initial emotional reactions evolve usefully in that space, too.

- **Express your initial thoughts and feelings**

  Get them down on paper or share with a friend. This will help your journey progress.

- **Avoid talking to any reviewers too early**

  If you are feeling totally OK with your feedback then you may talk with your reviewers, but if you have not reached this stage yet then wait until you do.

- **Avoid reaching firm conclusions too early**

  You may want to work it out and decide what is behind your data quickly, but you will get more out of it if you generate hypotheses first. Note them down and this will give you space for a deeper level of understanding.

- **Avoid drafting an action plan too early**

  If something is "wrong" it is easy to want to fix it straight away, but the best results come when there is time for reflection and coaching. Set yourself a target date, say a month away, by when you want to be clear on your action plan.

- **Don't do it alone**

  If it is just you looking at your data then you will only get so far in understanding and gaining the possible insights. It is advisable to ensure you have support and an experienced coach or manager to help you work through your data. This sharing with someone is a crucial part of the acceptance process, although this is not necessarily easy data to deal with so pick your person with care.

Once you have read your feedback, the next thing to do is to check you have perspective. Emotions will seriously get in the way of you ever seeing the data. You may think that is an exaggeration, but many a time have I seen someone letting their emotions go and only then spotting details and highlights previously invisible. It is totally normal to look for the bad stuff and then, when you have seen it, to ignore all the rest of the data. Neuroscience now shows us that this really happens[4]. As the psychologist **Rick Hanson**[5] has said, *"The mind is like Velcro for negative experiences and Teflon for positive ones."* Negative thoughts have our brains stick in particular places. Additional positive thoughts make no impact on this activity - as if they have no power when there are stronger, more compelling thoughts around. This tendency may be useful for survival, but it does not necessarily leave you clear on the whole picture or happy with your future.

To help you manage your emotions, release these reactions in a constructive and safe way and aim to relook at your data thoroughly and calmly. Be sure to really look at all the positive pieces and to look for the positive sides to those bits of feedback you may consider as "negative".

You may be seen as a bit abrupt and sharp at times, but this may have a clear advantage in getting things finished and bringing pace and energy. Find someone to help you see these positives if you cannot spot them. There is something positive in every single piece of feedback. You just might have to work hard to spot it.

Get really clear about what you do not like in your feedback. Highlight it or make a separate note. Once you have written it down it will start to move into being more manageable. You may still feel upset. There are some common reasons for feeling upset about feedback and it is useful to look at these and see which applies to you - it may be one, some or all!

- **Unfulfilled expectation**
- **Unexpressed communication**
- **Unappreciated contribution**
- **Disrespected strengths or style**

Having had the experience of giving 360° feedback to over 500 people, I am now clear that every upset can be unpicked. You cannot make the data disappear and you cannot make relations or opinions better than they actually are right now, but you can transform your response and perspective to these relationships and you can take on new strategies for the future. You can drop feeling upset about the things you do not like and you can shift from a perspective of *"This is definitely wrong"* to something more useful like *"This is a challenge and it will take something new to shift it"*. It is also clear that anyone can hold on to their upset or grievance literally forever and that many people need help to be OK.

A complicating issue lying within your data is the stereotypes or biases your reviewers are bringing to the process. Spotting the stereotypic influences will be hugely enlightening and useful. This may allow you to unpick all your upsets in one go! But it is tricky to see these as you will have detailed ratings and opinions about you, personally. How are you to know where these opinions have come from? However, there are some tricks to spotting prejudicial influences. First, look at the range and alignment of views. If there are commonly held opinions then there could be a commonly held stereotype at play. Consider which biases may be impacting you and find out how such bias would affect the feedback if it were there. Common gender bias[6] patterns can be seen to show men as more likely to be seen as driven, commercial and strategic; women to be seen as more organised and better at relating. If you are a woman who is very driven and not that organised then consider that your style might be working against your stereotype and that might lead to a little confusion, disappointment or lack of respect. Reviewers may not be as impressed with your drive as they would be if your gender were different. This will show up in your data as surprisingly lacklustre feedback where you might expect glowing positives. Being counter-stereotypical or counter-cultural in style has its consequences. It can lead people to feel you are not quite right or that they cannot quite trust you. Fitting the norm has an easy feel to it. Breaking the norm is tough work, for you and for everyone else.

A specific example of how stereotypes can impact you is in the ability to be frustrated at work. It has been recently identified that women are not really "allowed" to express their dissatisfaction as freely as men, which effectively limits the options available to women. Research by **V. L. Brescoll and E. L. Uhlmann**[7] concluded that men who expressed anger in a professional context were conferred higher status than those men who expressed sadness and, more critically, an angry female professional was conferred lower status (and lower wages) than an angry man. Women's emotional reactions were attributed to internal characteristics, e.g. *"She's out of control"*, *"She's over-emotional"*, whereas men's emotional responses were attributed to external circumstances. The consequences of this finding are profound and lead to women feeling they have to be unemotional in order to be acceptable and rational. An effective alternative, however, is for women to offer external, situational explanations for anger. This trend will not bother you if you are a man, or you are woman and things are going well but if, as a woman, you are noticing that things could be going better, this prejudice will be impacting you profoundly and painfully. Possibly invisibly, too.

Clues about a stereotypic influence include non-specific comments and ratings that are not backed up with clear examples. Opinions that are not quite fitting with people's experience of you give the game away, too. Look for what you might consider to be an unbiased view - someone from outside the company or sector. Look at the facts about you, and your achievements or credentials, and see if your data matches these. Look for tell-tale comments such as "*He doesn't fit in here*", or "*For a Yorkshireman...*", or "*She is impressive for such a tiny woman*". Usually though there are no explicit comments to give it away. These days people are supremely conscious of their language and, in addition to this, most of our bias is totally hidden from our consciousness anyhow.

Stereotypes affecting you may well take some seeking out, then. Here is a list of some potentials for you to consider. The usual list is deliberately mixed up with less publicised items, and my own specifics are provided so that examples later in the book make sense:

Gender	Female
Height	Tall
Accent	Southern English with a hint of Geordie and Brummie
Sexuality	Heterosexual
Dress sense	Professional, elegant, classic with a hint of playful "gamine"
Religion	Church of England, high Anglican
Shoes	Elegant heels, bit worn
Ethnic origin	British
Accessories	Wooden, angular, medium-sized
Skin colour	Caucasian

Academic background	Degree and post-graduate, University of Bristol
Schooling	Girls' grammar
Car	Old pale blue Jaguar XF
Poshness	Medium, depends on your perspective
Prettiness	Not particularly
Communication style	Clear, calm and enthusiastic
Function/department	MD
Professional perspective	HR and Occupational Psychology
Hair colour	Medium brown/auburn
Work experience	11 years in HR followed by 22 years of Occupational Psychology consulting, plus running own business for 16 years; two years in US
Out of work achievements	Church bell-ringing record-holder, set up and ran a choir
Hairstyle	Changes from shortish to longer and curlyish
Health	Varying, have had broken bones, pneumonia and serious chronic issues, including pesticide poisoning
Body shape	Thin, long limbs
Age	Mid-50s
Children	Three
Voice tone	Mezzo-soprano, can be loud
Outside work interests	Church bell-ringing, singing, personal transformation, natural childbirth and homeopathy
Exceptional achievements	Author of a book
Politics	Middle ground
Disability	None until I fractured my kneecap!

Each of these form facts about you. You cannot change them. Some of these are totally visible and cannot even be hidden from view. Others you may not tell anyone about, though. They all impact how you come across to other people. The fact and the label bring other connections and other opinions. While I was writing this list I realised I often omit to mention my interest and training in homeopathy. There is a reason for my hesitation! I may wish sometimes to look more powerful or authoritative, but I do not consider changing my body shape to something sturdier, although my build probably does impact me and my relations significantly.

Do consider your own answers to this list and reflect on which factors are impacting you and which may be influencing your reviewers, and therefore your feedback. The chances are that all of these factors are, indeed, having an impact. Highlight which are the three biggest ones for you and highlight also those you can change. Note that you can gain more qualifications, minimise bits of your past if you want, keep quiet about your politics, adjust your dress and your hair, work on your communication style and promote or simply gain more outside interests and achievements. There is actually plenty you can work with here, but there is also plenty (about half of the list) that you cannot change without serious surgery or major denial - they are worth understanding and owning as these stereotypes may be running the show, like having a continual background noise of a bathroom fan permanently switched on.

Your feedback is supposed to be about you. On the face of it this is true but there are other things at play. Bias and expectation, i.e. other people's stuff, has a large influence and it is useful to see if you can spot what of your feedback is connected to the stereotypes that impact you and what is outside of that. Whether the opinions are formed from a generic stereotype or not, they are all coming from the label that your reviewers have put on you or the box they have put you in. These identifiers are there as soon as you see or hear of someone and they seriously limit what is possible for you, and yet at the same time they empower you to do what is expected. The key is to see that they are there, influencing you now and in the future, and this book has been written to support you through this understanding so you can be conscious, powerful and free in managing your personal box or brand inside of these prejudicial influences.

CHAPTER 2

You are not an isolated being

"Reality is merely an illusion, albeit a very persistent one"

A Einstein

You know who you are. You know lots about you, and more than anyone else. Or do you?

There are, indeed, many things you know about yourself. It may be hoped that, as you get older and more experienced in life, this knowledge increases. Thank goodness! But there are many, many things you do not know. If you knew everything there was to know you would never be surprised, you would be in full control of what you do and how you feel, surely. You would have things worked out exactly as you planned - why ever not? But your own responses to things emerge mysteriously at times. Your intentions are not always met 100%. You seem to cause unexpected reactions in other people. Things do not always go to plan.

It is clear that your brain is very elastic, that your hormonal balances shift and adjust continually, and your desires and ambition alter over time as well. In fact, your energy and sensitivity can be altered simply by someone angry or upset entering the room. You are not a static machine. And then there are the others.

Other people do not necessarily understand you fully, if at all. They can easily get you "wrong", in your eyes, and judge you harshly. They may not be open to your leadership. A useful way of looking at this is to see that there are things we know about ourselves, and there are things we do not know. Other people also know stuff about us and there is also a heap of things they do not know. They may know you are tall, slim and well-spoken. They know how you appear, they know how you make them feel, they know how they see you communicate and they make a range of conclusions about you based on these observations and the facts they know about you. But they do not know what your real intentions are or about those feelings you keep to yourself. They do not know why they feel this way about you or what is really going on in the dynamic between you. The **Johari Window**[8] (below) describes this clearly.

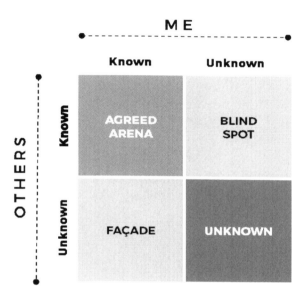

The agreed arena is what everyone is aware of. People around you know you are tall and slim and personable, for instance; they know you are usually enthusiastic, positive and energetic, and can be funny and creative at times. That's why they enjoy being in the pub with you! This you can see as part of your reputation and your current brand. It will show up clearly in your 360° as the data will show general agreement and alignment. There are always aspects you cannot see, though, just as your vision has a blind spot and needs the support of mirrors. Drivers of the brand-new invention, the car, 100 years ago, drove without mirrors, but the dangers soon became apparent! In 1909, **Dorothy Levitt** noted in her book, *"The Woman and the Car"*, that women should carry a little hand mirror in a convenient place when driving, and hold it aloft from time to time in order to see behind. A fixed rear-view mirror first appeared in the Indy races in 1911, but it was not until 1968 that a rear-view mirror became obligatory. You literally cannot see the back of yourself without a clever mirror and you cannot see how you are truly impacting everyone without help. How can you be fully present in the moment, dealing with all your thoughts and feelings whilst simultaneously listening and looking at everyone else in the room understanding their every thought and feeling? It is simply not possible. Acute observers and skilful therapists can attempt to pick up people's response, but most of us are not as well-trained or even interested... and it is impossible to know accurately how people a distance from you, e.g. the other side of the boardroom table, Twitter, your blogs or media coverage, are affected by your actions. Skilful PR and communications professionals will be able to take a good guess, but again it is not easy. You therefore have blind spots and these are well worth looking to expose and see. Why would you drive only being able to see in front of you when you can easily see behind, too?

Other people know what they know about you. Depending on how well you know them and their general level of accuracy of judgement of you, there will be stuff they do not know about you. They may know you as tall, slim and enthusiastic, but they do not know your full background and they do not your capabilities. You may turn up eagerly and positively, so others may assume you are happy to be there, that you love your work and that you are ambitious, but you may not be. You may be fed up, bored and rather wishing you could find a new challenge somewhere else. Others have opinions and thoughts about you, fed by stereotypic observations or by you. At a simple level, others do not get you - you are operating under a façade or a cover up.

This dynamic of facts and assumptions and how they feed opinions of you can be seen by an updated Johari window below:

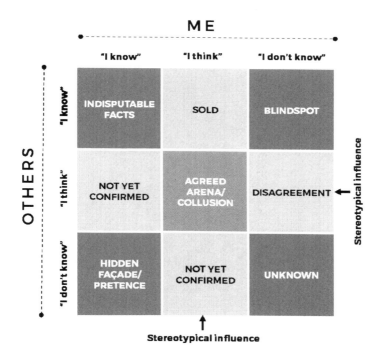

Overleaf is a completed example, with the responses (in italic capitals) very kindly provided by my 12-year-old son to these questions:

- *"What do you know about me?"*
- *"What do you think about me?"*
- *"What do you not know about me?"*

A façade or cover-up has its consequences. Things go more smoothly if people around you understand you better. Pretending to be coping at work when, in fact, you are stressed, for instance, can carry some risks.

Looking like you are organised when you are forgetful and chaotic can lead people to feel neglected when this is not your intention.

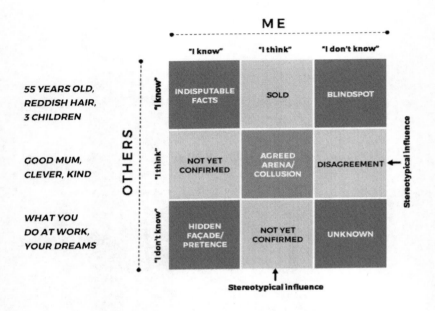

You and everyone else have no real idea what is possible for you or what is coming in the future. Despite us generally wanting to know stuff in life, the truth is that you do not. Anything is possible.

It appears clear now that the better you know and understand yourself, the better your effectiveness and success will be. Apart from intuitively thinking it is good to grow and expand yourself, recent evidence of this is shown in research by **Cornell University's School of Industrial and Labor Relations**[9] which found that a high self-awareness score was, in fact, the strongest predictor of leadership.

However well-formed our self-identity is, it is always the perfect fit to the sense and history of who we are to ourselves. If you are tall and slim and a friendly church bell-ringer then it fits that you are a little different, popular and non-cool. You are very attached to your self-image. It is precious and you love it, or love to hate it, whatever fits your story.

There will be things in your self-image that you like and things that you don't like so much but they are all your friends and will be hard to let go. After all, your whole story could unravel! But they may not be as meaningful and factually based as you imagine. It is your attachment to these characteristics of your self-image that can cause you to feel upset when you get your feedback. Consider the worst eventuality - something you love about yourself is totally ignored or not believed. For instance, in my mind I was nice and personable, liked by most, but I moved to work in the US and discovered after a few months that no one liked me. The whole team thought I was snooty, detached and aloof. Shocking! Why might this happen? Well, Americans may "like" the British accent, but generally consider the English to be... you guessed it... snooty, detached and aloof. It's the history and the accent and a bunch of other generationally-inherited things, at a guess. It is possible also that it is connected to the tendency for the Brits to be more compliant, organised and planful combined with the snooty sound a British accent has to an American ear. There are broad cultural stereotypes affecting people's opinion. Moving cultures or companies can suddenly bring such biases to light, but they are there all the time. My personableness was deeply precious to me until this experience but I then, in my moment of pain, decided to drop the need to be nice and liked and got on with things. The result was a more free, more powerful and funnier version of me - as if a layer of "niceness" had gone. Your special characteristics and beliefs about yourself may seem critical to your happiness, but the truth is that no characteristic is actually crucial for survival - although it still takes courage to drop them.

You know who you are and you have a strong sense of "good" and "bad" about such characteristics. When you consider personal characteristics, i.e. those aspects that differentiate people, occasionally there is a neutrality about it. More often, though, you are clear which you prefer, which would really be better in most circumstances, which you would rather be. Even "personality" traits that are said to be "neither good nor bad" can lead you to a sense of preference. You might buy the argument that extroversion and introversion are opposites and either is fine, but you know which you think you are and which you would rather be - unless you consider yourself in the middle, in which case the middle place may be where you prefer. This sense of judgement may be small and it may be unconscious, but you probably know how you would like to be.

This self-judgement is a critical part of self-esteem. You know who you are and you know you are OK (or not). That leaves you feeling positive and comfortable with yourself. Our judgements generally are useful and critical for full functioning. You will be making an estimated 35,000 conscious decisions each day (a child makes about 3,000) just in normal life. This number may sound absurd, but in fact, we make approximately 227 decisions each day on just food alone, according to researchers at Cornell University[10]. Processing is extremely fast. MIT neuroscientists found in 2014 that the human brain can process entire visual images in only thirteen milliseconds[11]. This level of decision-making has to be done in the background, you do not have enough time in your conscious thought to deal with them all. So you are a fast judgement machine and many of these judgements inevitably build in observations or information from the past and/or from other people. You soak them up. You will experience the judgements of your family and your upbringing through what is vocalised and what is done. The sense of "good" and "bad" will be there for you to accept or to rebel against.

You are likely to think that your sense of "good" and "bad" is right. That is the whole point of this judgemental process! You may think that anyone else in their right mind would think so, too. But it is when you have a taste of a very different culture that you can see that these judgements can emerge and sustain very differently. In Britain, for instance, it is good to greet people politely and say "hello" and "how are you?" or some other age-appropriate follow-up, but in Japan I suspect this would be "bad". The Japanese bow their heads in politeness and hold their hands together.

Even when you have just completed a purchase in a shop. In Britain it would be OK to walk to the station in heels, but in the US it might be considered rather stupid and impractical (judging from the lack of sympathy I got when I fell and twisted my ankle in Boston!).

Why might such differences emerge? History plays a big part, of course, but it is also about differences in values. There is always a good reason why people do things - it is always right for them, so different behaviours will have different values underlying them. A culture that is more abrupt will have speed and results as important, for instance; a culture that has beauty as important will value design over practicality. Take note of offices of arts-focused organisations. This is a game of mine. I have noted a lift that looks at least 100 years old (with manual door sliding mechanism), chairs in the reception that are virtually impossible to sit in, lifts left not working, computer systems going down every day. This is not what you see in technical, financial or engineering-type company offices.

It is very important to be true to your values and to know and appreciate your values. Being authentic and aligned really works. But, at the same time, you will necessarily and automatically be undervaluing other values.

You are in a world of comparisons. You like to compare and judge other people. You like to get clear as to how you compare to others, whether you see yourself as competitive or not. You will be interested to know how your 360° data compares to others' data, for instance. Is it good or bad? You always need a benchmark, it is part of calibrating yourself, feeding your own self-image further. Consider what life and work would be like if comparisons were not made, or if they were, it made no difference and had no impact? It would potentially take a bit of the interest out of it. Our planet has only a finite amount of land and a growing world population so perhaps this naturally leads to a sense of competition. Or maybe in our search for a purpose we look to comparisons to make the game of life interesting. There are levels of consciousness and development that mean you may sit above such comparisons, but this is not the case for the majority.

You do not just like to compare, you like to win, to be on the side that is "good", even if you do not see yourself as competitive. You may feel that you are not winning and you might think this does not apply to you, but you may also see that you always win at the game you are playing. Whether this "game" is the one that involves trying really hard and not getting very far, or the one that ends up with you suffering and needing help, or the one that means you are the star that wins after years of determination. Achieving a result can sometimes lead you to feel neutral or disappointed rather than the expected celebration. Such examples can show you how complex this issue may be. Your winning may not fit with your self-identity. Nevertheless, this social calibration is part of humanity. You may know people who have given this "game" up, but the option to give up is also part of the game.

You may not agree with this view of life, but the point is that you are in a world of comparisons and other people's opinions impact you. Unless you have taken an unusual course of action, e.g. to enter a reclusive and solitary existence, you are in a social environment. There have been a few films recently showing what life could be like totally on your own. You would be a rare person to be immediately and obviously happy in a solitary condition. You need people, but people come with their opinions. You are likely to be gathering and working with other people with similar values as you, as that also is the human condition, but you will inevitably come across others assessing you from a different mindset from your own. As you progress to become more senior, your position will be more and more different from those under you in the organisation. You will start to differ from them in terms of age, experience, skill and authority.

It is not just a simple process of you needing to understand others' opinions or insulating yourself from them. It is more complex than this, as others' opinions help form you.

You and your development will be influenced by the judgements you live with. Some of these opinions will be empowering and build you up, some will be neutral and others will disempower you. Opinions will reinforce what you already know about yourself or they might start to change your mind, and the opinions will be culturally dependant. It becomes a circular or dynamic process, which results in the maintenance of communities and cultures. An example shows how this works. As mentioned earlier, when I was in the US I did not like being seen as aloof and superior, so developed mechanisms to manage and compensate for this. Then I came across some Brits who had lived in the US for over ten years. They told me clearly that I should maintain my British accent carefully as it will be very important to do so. They did not mind being aloof and superior. When I thought about it, I could remember them being exactly that way back in England! So, something different happens if you naturally fit your stereotype.

If you have ever worked for a boss who thought you were good and had great potential, you will know what it feels like to be at the receiving end of positive opinions. It can bolster and feed, encourage and support your courage and development. The positive psychology movement has emphasised the advantages of working within a context of positivity and a focus on strengths rather than on the "weaknesses". More recently, research is showing us that objective assessment of performance and appraisal has significant limits and indicates again that positivity makes more positive difference to people and to results[12]. Positive practices include inspiring one another, emphasising meaningfulness, treating one another with respect, gratitude, trust and integrity.

But it is the case that any opinion has advantages and disadvantages. Opinions are inevitable and impactful and the rest of this book helps explain how to really know what they are and what to do with them if you decide they are unhelpful to you. If you see yourself as a nice cuddly cat out for an easy, cosy life, yet others around you see you as someone having dangerous claws worth being scared of, then it is worth knowing and it is worth having a clear strategy for dealing with it.

CHAPTER 3

Opinions are logical, but not objectively formed

You make judgements all the time, every second of every waking hour. They are made fast. You decide what to think, what to do, what to say, what to feel, how to move and how to digest, breathe, divert your immunity and direct your blood. I remember the enormity of the responsibility of all of this dawning on me when I was about six years old, when I asked my mother *"When do I have to make my heart pump myself?"* and I got the answer, *"Now and forever."* I felt pretty burdened with that idea! Thankfully only a small proportion of these decisions are conscious, with the rest happening without us knowing. Thankfully so, because otherwise we would have to have life be very simple to cope, there would simply and literally be too much to think about. But this cleverly automated processing has a downside when it comes to the subtlety of assessing yourself and other people. Most of us are complex individuals and require complex understanding for any degree of sophisticated knowledge. However, as a result of being structured as you are, you function with simplicity to assess and judge a complex phenomenon. The surprising and confusing aspect to this is that you, along with most of humanity, do not realise this!

The process of categorisation comes in to guide and give you the simplicity you need. It is thought that, as you grow and develop through childhood and adulthood, you build a complex map of categorisation with which you can assess people. You adopt this from the map you find yourself in your family, your school and local community, your peers and your enemies. You accept some and you rebel and refuse others. It took me quite a while to realise that my family's (and possibly also my country's culture) categorisation of rich people - where those with lots of money were somehow "bad" and those with less were "better" - was unhelpful. Once I had dropped that categorisation for myself I found I had more freedom to earn and strive, etc. I then had to deal with the trickiness of spending money in a family that did not approve of such spending. Having said that, this was nothing compared to the trickiness of marrying into a family from North Yorkshire who did not just despise money, but also London, the South-East and mothers who had careers!

It is through categorisation that you learn how to deal with people. Most of the time it is not a simple need to know if you face danger, as it may once have been. *"Are you friend or foe?"* is the basic issue that it deals with. But it then allows you to work out how to befriend someone, to decide whether you want to have dealings with them, whether they can help you, whether you should help them, how to make sure they do not aggravate or get in your way, how to enjoy them. It seems that what categorisation does really well is allow you to manage your boundaries and your safety. That is what it is designed to do so it is not surprising. Where categorisation falls down badly is in leading you to close your mind about people, to put them in a "box" and give them a label which will inevitably lead you to see them more narrowly than before. Possibilities may be totally unseen. Again, though, this is not surprising as the job of categorisation is to allow you to manage yourself, not to bring broad and creative possibilities to the world!

You have an ability to function with categorisation that may be out of date with what you are needing and wanting in today's life. Yet you probably relate to your categories and their resulting judgements of others as if they are right and totally defensible. Let's explore this further. If you were to categorise people fully and accurately then you would have to gather lots of data on them over a period of time and from a range of angles and different contexts and measures. This is certainly what an occupational psychologist aims to do when "assessing potential", for instance. It takes something to gather the evidence and to have the expertise to make such an assessment and, even with the latest in psychometrics and work simulation methods, while it may give you clarity on how someone will perform in certain conditions and how they compare against a relevant benchmark, it will still only be a glimpse of today's individual doing an assessment. Even if you were to leave the assessment to the individual themselves or a boss who has managed them for years, you will still only understand a portion of this individual and virtually nothing about what is possible for them in the future. With the functioning capacity we have at the moment we are limited as a human race; it is not personal to you but common to all of us.

You need to know what to think about someone, yet it is seemingly impossible to really know. The inevitable result of this conundrum is that you make judgements based on categories. It is inevitable then, with the fast speeds involved, that there will be prejudice, i.e. prejudging, based on appearance or facts. What is obvious about someone will form those initial connections in your brain. This is probably why the biases in skin colour and gender are so high in the political agendas. You cannot easily change your gender or skin colour, yet they work in those first few seconds.

You can tell if your assessments of people are based on a "bias" or instead on a thinking assessment by looking at the speed of your thinking. You cannot spot or assess the speed differences in normal life but you can in experimental conditions such as that developed by Harvard scientists with others. Do have a go at these free tests to see how biased you currently are[13]. Categorisations and biases filter our perceptions and our view of the world and of specific people. That is their job. Once you have decided someone is potentially difficult, you will inevitably see their behaviour through this judgement. Just as you might put sunglasses on... at first the world appears more brown than it did, but only seconds later this is forgotten and you are simply seeing the world as it is. Your brain adapts cleverly, makes it simpler for you, and assumes the filter. You are left with the experience that all is just as it should be. Your filters are there, but forgotten - until you remember to take your sunglasses off, when the world is suddenly very sharp and bright. The issue is that we have all got many, many sunglasses on and have totally forgotten about them!

All of this makes sense if you know that your perception is not accurate. The more we learn about visual stimuli, the more the tricks of our brains can be exploited. There are new advertising displays coming which use such technology, and that only show the whole graphic when you move your eye across it. Amazing and space saving!

You might wish to have a clear view and firm handle on the shape of your world but the more we understand about such matters, the more it seems you have no clue at all. I may think that I am clearly delivering my writing commitment on a laptop at a desk looking through shutters at the passing people, but an alternative interpretation might be that I am delivering my purpose and expressing myself with joy, the understanding is flowing and a new way is being created. Same facts, different assessment and totally different interpretation.

The "**Repertory Grid**" method of competency analysis, underpinned by the work of **George Kelly** and his **Construct Theory**[14], allows you to see how people are truly judging others[15].

Your view of your world is determined by you and impacted significantly by your experience and your upbringing, and also by your genetic and cultural inheritance. It is yours, yet it probably does not feel like you have full control over it. Far from it. All of this means that there is no such thing as "objectivity" when that is what most of us have been aiming for: **objectivity:** i.e. "*not influenced by personal feelings or opinions*"[16] as against **subjectivity:** i.e. "*dependent on the mind or on an individual's perception for its existence*"[16]. My belief is that there are not two different constructs after all, but only conscious judgement and unconscious judgement.

Objectivity is a worthy aim as it reflects the intention and aim to rise above your biases, but it is nevertheless an impossible goal and perhaps we should stop pretending that it is possible and be more real. Perhaps we should aim for "conscious evaluation" and a mature, thinking management of our opinions.

Being "biased" or "prejudiced" is considered "bad" in many cultures and communities. A bias in itself! The truth is that we are all biased and we are filtering people in many, many ways and most of the time we have no clue. You could aim to be OK with this and to be open and present, willing to question and look at your thoughts and your judgements instead.

So, you and everyone else have many opinions and prejudices, but how moveable are they? Pretty fixed is the short answer, but let's explore further. It now seems to be clear that our brains are very plastic, more plastic than we might imagine. Work with post-stroke patients shows how a permanently damaged brain can develop and grow connections so that the area and functions that have been lost are effectively worked around. It takes a lot of effort and continual work to have these new connections and replacement functionality, but it is possible. New muscular neurologist techniques also show how it is possible to encourage the body to reconnect where it had stopped functioning fully. Surely then you can change your opinions? If we follow the same process then it will take intention, intervention and repeated practice to maintain. Totally possible. Just like you might be skiing and decide to take a new run down a mountain... it takes something to choose a brand new track and it also takes a lot for the original tracks to disappear altogether and to be replaced by the new.

In the case of a neural loss of function you will have the desire to walk, etc., to help you progress and even this is not always enough. But the issue in the case of opinions is that there is a lot keeping them in place and it can be very unclear what you might get out of changing your mind. There is a process of "justification", i.e. the action of showing something to be right or reasonable[17], going on all the time and a post-event rationalisation, not to mention projection onto others. Things normally happen a bit like this: this occurred, you thought this and did the other and this was the result. If you look at this harshly, you might see that your perception and your opinions impact and affect literally each one of these steps. The end result is seeing that every one of your experiences has been formed by you and your filters, and that is before you factor in the fact that your filters impact how you are with others, which in turn impacts those others in a self-fulfilling way. So your stories and experiences back up your prejudices. No surprise there, but you may also start to see that there are many reasons why you should hold on to those opinions. If you were to change your opinion about someone, your previous judgements would then have been "wrong" and your experiences and stories that form your past would need to be rewritten to make sense. That takes something! You like to be right about your opinions, of course you do. You also like to be right about how and what happened in the past. You like to know, to understand and for the whole thing to make sense.

Apart from categorisation, there is another major phenomenon that impacts this opinion-forming process. The exception rule kicks in when an individual shows up who challenges your preconceptions and prejudice. Men might be expected to be seen as less effective at respect and managing activities than women,[18] but a man can show up who is super sensitive, fantastic in all areas of relationships and great at organising, too! You may be surprised at this when you meet this man and may even question why and whether he really is this way but, if the evidence is strong, then you will end up clear that this is how he is. He breaks your prejudice but you do not start to question your bias, instead you label him as an "exception", maintaining the bias exactly as it was. You may think that you cannot trust teenagers with money but one that comes along who is responsible and mature is the exception. You will only allow them to be an "exception" if the evidence is clear and strong, though. This connects with the common experience of women, for instance, who report that they have to try harder than men to get the same result. Being different from the commonly-held bias takes effort and continued energy. And it may impact your own personal position but it will not change the bias.

The other phenomenon that occurs as a result of the energy that is required to challenge a bias is that people avoid taking on characteristics that are counter-trend. Controlling women were not valued in my community and family so I was clear I was not going to be a bossy boss. I have been managing more than ten people for the last thirty years and it is hard to manage by never being bossy. I have had to learn how to really own and lead with authority from this position and it has not been easy. Women who are more naturally and easily bossy than me often develop different strategies to allow this characteristic to be fully integrated into their style.

All of this, though, is still working around the issue that it is not really allowed.

Not only does the exception rule mislead us but also there is the "not" categorisation phenomenon. If you do not like or fit into the obvious categorisation people are giving you, e.g. you do not relate to being a "man" or a "Southerner", then one strategy available is to decide that you are a "not man" or a "not Southerner". This means you are not relating to your category as being true to you, but you are also not relating to the opposite category or another specific category - you are simply not one of those! For others to see you in this way you will need to display something clearly. In my case I was only somewhat a "not woman" for a while, which showed up as my not hanging out with other women but preferring male activities such as bell-ringing and drinking pints of real ale. I continue to be a "non-Southerner" because there some values and connections with the "South" I did not connect with when I moved south at the age of seven. I show this by continuing a tinge of Geordie in my accent. With this sort of manoeuvring around the biases you can see how prejudices maintain as they are. Anything that challenges them gets managed or justified out of the way, and that's just the start of this self-fulfilling process.

So prejudices are tricky to change but opinions can be changed. We can see this in the world of public health. One of the first adverts on the new "television" talking about the dangers of smoking was replayed the other day. It was made in 1964, but it was not until the mid-1980s that smoking declined to the 30% level. We can learn from the world of brand management how it can be done. It takes real investment and intention, long-term campaigns and strategies. It is not short-term. It might take changes in products or services to signal a new approach, new laws or taxes, and, unless issues are dealt with, it may be easier to give up and a start a new brand instead!

To change your mind about someone you need a reason. Something needs to look different, be different, something new needs to be offered or said, something new needs to be felt or heard by others, you need to have a new and different impact. If this continues over a period of time then it is possible. But, given there is so much holding current opinion in place, it is still not guaranteed.

CHAPTER 4

Changing a stereotype is very hard to do

One of the inevitable consequences of the exception rule is that you alone cannot prove it wrong. The exception rule, as described earlier, occurs when you are seen as different from the bias or stereotype. It gives others permission to think that you are different, it justifies their unexpected views about you and allows you to be considered "intelligent and inspiring", for instance, when some big factors about you tell them you should not be this way. This is how people work and this is something you can use to help yourself. You can build on the fact you are "different" and reinforce your own individual characteristics. If you are clear and proud and able to laugh at yourself then it will sustain and become a key part of the reputation you can develop.

If you want to challenge the stereotype that impacts you and your kind then, as many women do at the moment for instance, then something significant has to happen that impacts the reality of the stereotypic basis. You have three options: you can either change the story to kill the type, overwhelm the defining facts with stronger messages or destroy the defining fact itself. All of these are hard to even imagine and very hard to achieve simply in order to change the bias, but of course they are all possible. Just consider the stereotype you have about the people of Wessex... anything come to mind? Probably not. The fact that Wessex was a kingdom in South-West England in Anglo-Saxon times and disappeared in the 10th century probably has something to do with this. You can be sure, though, that during the 9th century there was a clarity in neighbouring kingdoms about what "Wessex girls" were like compared to them! But today we don't have a living bias for or against Wessex girls. Something has to happen that rocks the current dynamics at play. Legal changes, policies on "equality and diversity", HR processes and procedures, targets for minorities at board level, etc., all sound like they would be useful and are clearly well-intentioned but they do nothing to shift the true value and comparisons at play. The behavioural economist, **Iris Bohnet,** has recently published the book "*What Works. Gender Equality by Design*" (2016), and this is strongly recommended reading to empower and guide changing such practices.

Evidence-based research sounds such a great idea. You can see it being referred to and valued in all sorts of areas these days. In medicine, HR, complementary health, practices in childbirth, etc., but if you ever get into the detail of new thinking and research the body of thinking yourself you may be surprised how slow and resistant current professionals and "experts" can be even to a vast body of respected evidence-based research. Always for a good reason, of course, but this shows how opinion and practice is not simply based logically on the evidence. Instead there are many complex and subtle influences at play that maintain positions. If that is the case then showing evidence and campaigning "against" positions is very unlikely to work and rarely can be seen to do so. Campaigning on the grounds of moral judgement might change what is seen as "right" and "wrong", but it may not touch the true beliefs and behaviour. Instead it can drive practices underground. I lived in the ancient merchant city of Bristol for years before I heard about the hidden passageways and cellars that had allowed slaves to move from ship to land without being seen. Subversive bias is no better than explicit, and possibly more harmful, as the resulting judgements and decisions may not be obviously biased and therefore are more likely to be taken personally.

It seems that the most pervasive and entrenched stereotypes are historically-based and intergenerational in origin. They come from a different age, one that we cannot fully understand from our viewpoint of today's world. How can you begin to understand the gender bias as it exists today without understanding what it was like to be a "woman" just two or three generations ago? My grandmother (born 1898) was only allowed to stay at school if she committed to being a teacher afterwards. She refused, left school at thirteen and became one of the first secretaries working the brand new-fangled typewriters on the railway. She knew she had to give up work when she got married. No question. My mother (born 1933) had four male and one female cousins. All the boys had private schooling funded by the grandmother; the two girls did not. She could work when she married, but she had to give up when she fell pregnant. Again, no question. I (born 1962) was one of the first in my generation to know I could work full-time and have children. Generational steps have definitely occurred, along with a new economic dynamic. Perhaps such big changes cannot happen within a generation. Each generation has to know they are making the right choices in life and that they are doing the "right" thing. It is very hard for anyone to accept that those hard-thought decisions were wrong. It is much easier to consider your approach to be the right one and to give permission (reluctantly, maybe) to later generations to do things differently.

The fact is that our brains do not normally get reprogrammed or rebooted. Our stories do not get rewritten unless there has been significant new insight and a transformational learning experience. *"What's in it for me?"* pertains and maintains. The dynamic that had the stereotypic influences exists until it has been destroyed. Hence perhaps why it is so deeply shocking how hard it is to change stereotypes.

The bigger dynamic at play that causes stereotyping to occur is the fact that the world is a forced comparison. Humanity loves to know what and who is better or worse. This becomes clear if you imagine what life might be like if, for instance, there were no bias referring to "gender". What might that look like? Gender could be one of the trickiest to fathom given almost all communities in the world include a combination of genders - for the obvious reason that procreation is critical for long-term sustainability. Shifts in the gender bias may not arise until men can easily have babies. Unfortunately, it is going to take a lot more than the transgender example of childbirth that reached the news in 2008.

So, comparisons between groups and communities, knowing how your "team" or "tribe" differs from others around you, is an important part of how you manage your own self-identity and sense of self-esteem. It is a vital and interesting part of how humanity operates. Resisting and minding this is going to be as useful as resisting death, one of those inevitable outcomes for all of us. It is going to be tiring, exhausting and a source of frustration and grief. A lot of effort is involved. But you can take action and campaign without frustration. Actions coming from a sense of "injustice" and moral wrongdoing has a certain look and feel, and can have strong and compelling arguments. Of course all people "should" have equal opportunities despite their colour, gender and sexuality, for instance. To try to argue against that these days you will position a particular group or label as better than another. Your consciousness will see the flaw in this argument but the main point is that your ability to be persuasive will be impacted by a sense of freedom and power on the subject. Taking a stand for fairness and equality is a more powerful position to speak from, rather than being angry and disappointed.

If you want to cause transformation then the first step is to be comfortable and relaxed about the situation, at the same time as being fully committed to a new future. Then you can access your full capacity as a leader, you can think creatively and can generate a team. You can see different ways to take people where you want to go and you will be able to expand your ability to engage and inspire others. You will be able to give others the choice to make up their own minds, to come with you or not, and they can own the choice and join you as a partner on the journey. You will then find that the goal and the journey becomes a shared co-creation and takes shape in a different way than you could possibly have imagined. This is transformational leadership. It is peaceful, powerful, committed and enthusiastic.

You will recognise where you are in relation to the categories you live with by how it feels to think about them. If there is a positive feeling and a lightness when you think about your category then you are in a good place; if there is a negative sense to your thoughts then there is work to do. There is acceptance to attain to - a bit like there is as you work through any "bad" news, as described in the grief response in chapter 1.

As you can see, the starting position is hearing the news in the first place, i.e. being conscious of it. In terms of stereotypes it has taken me many years to truly see, feel and hear the extent (or the detail) of the gender stereotype, for instance. I operated as a woman in male-dominated businesses (starting with the finance, security, manufacturing and motor industries) without realising the extent of the dynamic at play, yet it clearly was impacting me and my ability to speak and lead every single day. There will be biases and stereotypes that are impacting you negatively every day, too. They might be more subtle, minor influences, but they might not be. HR people, for instance, usually have no idea how badly they are impacted by simply being "HR". All of us are impacted by age, for instance - either by being "too young" to know stuff or by being "too old" to be important. I still remember the very moment I first heard someone refer to me as "posh". To me I was the northern, non-posh one in a Home Counties town, and then a grammar school girl amongst others from private schools at university. Others were posh, not me! It was my first real HR job in a manufacturing plant in "Brimsdown" (a name that felt apt!), North London. It took a while to realise I was not only the most senior woman on a site of 450 diverse characters at the same time as being the least well paid in the managerial grades, but also that I was actually the highest qualified on site (bar the R&D director). And my accent was totally posh to all these people. With this came with a slight distrust and detachment which I overcame through determined charm and constructive support and work. First, though, I had to be OK with being posh.

A healthy perspective on this matter is to assume you have no clue and start to look more carefully and curiously and be ready to spot new biases you had not previously seen. As you get older and more senior in your career you will find your wisdom and experience will get in the way of your relating with others more junior, for instance, way beyond what you might imagine to be reasonable. Be ready and be alert. Seeing the biases and looking at them as being connected to your community and your generational inheritance is a part of this acceptance process. A bias impacting you negatively feels personal and it is indeed about you personally, yet it is never truly personal to you.

The key thing to do about a bias you have spotted and you do not care for is to drop minding. I remember spotting with horror that my girlfriends at secondary school thought my hobby of bell-ringing was a bit "nerdy", definitely uncool. The cool girls made this super clear! Given I was fairly well hooked and fascinated by this mathematical and team-oriented musical instrument by then, I was not going to give up. I tried not talking about it. That was OK and felt a bit safer but, of course, it leaks out and the nerdy label sticks. I shrugged it off and decided to enjoy it and then started writing up my strange "methods" on the blackboard at every opportunity. I laughed at their mockery and laughed with them at myself and generally enjoyed being quirkily different. I had freedom to do what I wanted, I did not have to be "cool" to be OK and soon became famous for my unusual bell-ringing. Friends started to join me and I have loved this aspect of my character ever since.

The sensation that frees you is a "giving up", a "letting go". Pick up your pen and hold it as if you are going to write with it. Now drop it. It is just like that. A simple act on your part but one that requires you to choose and engage, to take an order and to move your fingers. The fact is that you can choose to hold on to your pen, your opinions and thoughts about something literally for ever. If you do then you must be getting something super-juicy out of it. Given it takes effort and energy to hold a pen, there must be something that makes it worthwhile for you. This is logical.

Why might you hold onto your issues and complaints about your stereotypes? Well, there is usually a lot of good stuff you can be "right" and opinionated about. Any injustice is supremely good to get self-righteous about. By minding your stereotype you are criticising those involved. They will not appreciate that! You get to dominate and have the upper hand, which automatically means others have the lower hand (if there is such a thing). Again, not a good result. You can continue to use your complaint as justification for things not working, for your own lack of results, for anything, really. The more you think about it, the more this simply does not seem worth it.

Once you have dropped that the bias is "wrong" a whole new realm is possible. A new space opens up and a fresh energy can be sourced and maintained. You can talk about it differently, probably with more freedom. You can share about it. You can offer support and you can question others on it. You can refer to it in the moment - or "call it out". You can be amused and you can laugh. You will be interested rather than outraged and expressive instead of sullen. New strategies can then emerge for you and you will find that your life expands in front of you.

CHAPTER 5

Your opinions of others impact you

Do your thoughts make you or do you make your thoughts? **Eckhart Tolle**[19] describes how our thoughts in childhood exist as energy forms, like entities, and get deeply lodged in our minds. We then identify with the thoughts as who we are. As Eckhart explains beautifully, the first moment of freedom comes when we realise we are not our thoughts. It is, of course, clear that you have opinions and you make judgements and decisions all the time, very fast and very often. It is also true that your experience of others and of life in general is impacted by the opinions you are referring to. Imagine turning up to work and thinking that everyone you work with is hopeless, ineffective and rather boring. You can just feel the weight of that experience! On the other hand, let's imagine that work has not changed and the people are the same, yet you are clear about how awesome they are, how committed, inspirational and determined. They care and their loyalty and sense of enthusiasm is palpable. That feels rather better, doesn't it? The fact is that your opinions of others impact your experience in the moment and in life in general.

These judgements are mostly going on in your head and you may think that they are private. They are, after all, only in your head, you do not speak of them - that would be rude! However, your opinions and thoughts will leak and at the same time be the filter through which you see and feel everything and everyone around you. You can distinguish between the negative and positive voices in your head. There are things you say in your head that empower you and other people and there are things that you say that undermine and destroy. They can be in direct contradiction with each other and they can co-exist happily, it seems. You can think other people are "not good enough" and "great" all at the same time!

Your thinking impacts your experience in the moment and also how the future unfolds for you. Visioning the future, imagining what it might look like and getting clear what you want are all well worth doing. Life without these processes is a certain way; if you then add this visioning you will start to feel you are living into a different future. It will drive and motivate you in a particular way. Given the power of your thoughts about the future on "now" then it stands to reason that you are advised to choose your future carefully. A friend of mine has a history of anxiety and depression and she shared with me the other day that she spent a lot of time imagining all the funerals that were likely to come up. This is akin to regular, negative self-hypnosis! There is a good reason why people who are managing someone who is very sick keep themselves going by saying "*I am taking just one day at a time.*" Perhaps the future is too hard to bear. I am more optimistic and spend time getting clear how I want my life to be. If I achieve my goal and then fail to redefine my future I can feel the difference in my motivation, here and now. After running my business for ten years I felt directionless and bored, even though I loved my work, my team and my company and it was going well. I suddenly realised one day that I used to have a vision of being MD of a successful business and wondered if I had simply ticked that off. I invented a new future and got clear what the next stage for me could be, and I was off again...

If you are not totally convinced about the power of your thoughts over today try this experiment: every morning when you wake up, say to yourself over and over, "*Humph, it's Monday morning,*" "*Oh no, it's Tuesday morning,*" etc. Take this on for two to three weeks. Then switch to saying to yourself, "*This is Monday, the best day of my life,*" "*This is Tuesday, the best day of my life.*" You have to generate it and believe it in the moment. Then it will go to work and guide your feelings and thoughts in the chosen direction. The results can be dramatic.

Thoughts seem to just happen. They come into your mind and they leave or they hang around. It can feel like you are not in control. Mindfulness and meditation can allow you some sense of ease and give you a practice so you are OK with not being in control, but you can consciously override these thoughts. You can manage them through actions and habits; through behaviours and through therapy. You can rewire your brain yourself if you are so inclined. It takes intention and commitment and a strong belief in your own power in the matter, but it is possible. Instilling new habits and new thoughts is perhaps the most useful and this takes concentrated effort and repeated actions. The best way to achieve such changes in personal habits is to invent new practices that you consider to be gorgeous, not things you "have to do" but that inspire and drive and motivate you. Something to run towards rather than turning away from. Be the master of your own destiny by managing your own constructive thinking. Build the life and effectiveness you want through managing your mind and your thinking habits.

Your thoughts affect your experience of life in every moment, but it is not just you that your thoughts impact, it is other people. Your opinions of other people impact you and impact them - in the moment and over a prolonged period of time. Do you have an idea of what others think of you? If so, then it stands to reason that others will pick up your opinions in return. Not that we are particularly accurate in understanding the subtleties of others' opinions - as the hundreds of 360° feedbacks showing sparse alignment of reviewers reminds me regularly. It is only the bold judgements, however, that show up very clearly and tend to be visible to everyone.

How do you tell what others think of you? There are many non-verbal clues that you pick up, if you have some degree of empathy, anyway. There are the micro expressions - "micro momentary" changes to the facial muscles[20]. There are the pupil movements of expansion and contraction, there is the body position, the mirroring and the mouth and many more possibilities that display emotions of anger, fear, disgust, happiness, sadness and surprise consistently across cultures. Expression of contempt seems less clear, which probably trips many of us up on our travels.

How close you stand to someone says something, as does the attention you give their speaking. There are many you may be aware of and many others you are likely to be unconscious of. The amount of time and energy you direct towards someone and the reactions to their arguments are perhaps the more obvious signs. It is the host of more subtle and indirect signals that can fool us. Your language and actions give it away, though, no matter how hard you might try to cover it up. There is always leakage in a cover-up situation and this can eventually lead to distrust and a sense of inauthenticity.

You might think you can always ask people what they think of you. For some this will work, but for many this will not give you what you are looking for. If someone is not telling you what they think of you there is a good reason why they keep it to themselves. They either think their opinion might be dangerous in some way if it were exposed or that expressing it would make no difference or even make things worse. These fears might have an accurate basis, but they might not. Nevertheless, tricky opinions will not get expressed easily. This fact is one of the reasons why 360° feedback can be so useful. It specifically and deliberately creates a process that gives people a safe way of expressing their views and opinions.

The most significant impact of others' opinions on you is not how you feel or react to their opinions in the moment or even how you respond to knowing their opinions. Something much more serious and significant happens - other people become what your opinion allows. If you think someone is useful and creative then you will expect this of them. The dynamic will result in the other person having the space and encouragement to come up with ideas and also for you to see these ideas as useful. This might end up being disproved but while your opinion is a certain way the other individual is actively supported and encouraged by your expectation and opinion. Your positive opinion literally makes them more likely to be useful and creative. For example, I was clear that I was not creative after my education. I was good at lots of things like maths, biology and psychology, and generally dealing with people, but I was not artistic or creative. An HR director boss thought I was, though. I disagreed but we did not argue about it. She simply kept giving me bigger and trickier projects to develop and deliver from scratch. They were innovative and collaborative and actually quite brilliant. One day I realised I was bold in my design and delivery because she believed I could do it. The word "creative" may not have been a label I related to, but she created an innovative and creative person through her opinion and confidence in me. I will be forever grateful.

This phenomenon of being created by someone else can be expansive or contracting for you. It can be conscious and unconscious. It is the "box" that others put you in. Consider some of the boxes people put you in. For me, I know others generally put me into the box that is labelled "woman, mother" with a sense of age that depends on *their* age. I am "middle-aged, i.e. old" to my boys, young to my father's generation and ageless to my peers. The box of "entrepreneur" or "business manager" does not hold strong for me even though it is equally valid. This is quite odd. As you can see, there is a hierarchy of labels that impacts the rigidity of the boxes. I am discovering the box "author" and will let you know how that one works in due course.

Conscious active impact can be seen when there is positive inclusion and invitations to take things on. This immediately builds participation and learning, and reinforces a positive view of you for yourself and the world at large. It makes a huge difference and happens all the time in the workplace. Consider whose views you ask for, who is asked to take things on, who is encouraged to speak up and who is allowed to present. This is empowering, unless it is a ploy for you to show your failings, of course.

Conscious active impact can also be seen when there is exclusion and a holding back from responsibility. Others being put forward rather than you means there is a net negative impact. Being ignored or avoided can feel "OK" but it should really be viewed as a put down. It is actually quite hard to see a neutral position and impact, in fact. If we look at the world of physics we can see that there is always momentum in one direction or another. Stasis in life may be what we would like, but it is not practically possible.

Unconscious impact will occur through the subtle empowerment or disempowerment of your communications. Imagine sharing a new idea you have with someone you know thinks you are amazing. You will present it energetically and with excitement. You feel comfortable that you will be heard and you will get a good hearing. You will deliver the message confidently and be happy to hear the response, whatever it is. Now imagine presenting the same idea to someone who thinks you are hopeless or less than good in some way. I was just thinking of a number of men in an older generation and now I cannot even be bothered to tell them my idea! You may hesitate because it feels like harder work and you may wait until you feel more confident about it. When you share your idea you are likely to deliver it with a little trepidation or alternatively perhaps some forcefulness, trying to persuade them of its merits. A totally different experience. You are a different version of you with these different views. Their opinions form you. Which means your opinions form others.

Where does this take you? It means you get to choose how other people are for you. If this is a new concept you might not quite believe it. Before dismissing this notion out of hand please do try an experiment or two. Pick someone you have decided is "grumpy" or something similarly negative. One day I focused on one of the ticket sellers at my local train station (the "grumpy" one!) and decided his grump impacted my experience of getting the train. I decided to consider him as a slightly lonely but committed guy wanting to serve all his customers efficiently. I put my phone away and asked for my ticket with care and speed. I then asked how he was coping with the cold and the ticket machine (that was always breaking down). He was friendly and helpful! He did not actually wish me a good journey but I felt like he did. Every time after that that he was grumpy I knew it was because I had not bothered to generate him as anything else. I got what I deserved.

This is the whole point - you get the people you create. Not only that... you then find that people turn into what you have created; your opinion becomes self-fulfilling. If you are clear that someone is wanting to help you then you approach them with that in mind and that expectation and speak to that commitment. In the moment of interaction it is actually quite hard for the other person to prove you wrong. You might notice that they are focused elsewhere or that they are struggling to do this, but they will find it hard not to end up helping you at some level. I remind myself of the power of my opinion on a regular basis with my husband in the area of care and help. He is a brilliant pure mathematician but not a natural "helper" or even a team player. He would be the first to admit. Just last night I was exhausted after presenting twice at a conference and was eating dinner very late with a tray on my lap brought in by my husband. I was really thirsty. My first thought was that he should have known I would need a drink. I have learnt now how far that gets me! I stopped myself and instead I tried, *"Darling, would you mind getting me a glass of water? I am so thirsty."* He stopped the TV, of course, and happily delivered the desired water. Result.

Every interaction with another is a subtle play and dynamic and if you are there you get an active role - always. You influence the interaction and the relationship and profoundly impact the other person. They act and feel inside the space and boundaries you give them. You act and feel inside the space they give you. The clearer your intention and the more positive it is, the bigger the impact you will have on "what happens". It is surprising how much you can affect people around you.

Shocking, actually. In the short term and long term there are opportunities to impact others and your relationships, although you cannot control the other person. Someone will not necessarily change who they are, but a positive and empowering opinion of other people can profoundly change how they relate to themselves and lead to sustained development and new behaviour. This leads us to the conundrum regarding change, which is that you can only truly change yourself and your thoughts and opinions but, by doing this, others will inevitably emerge differently and transform in front of your eyes. Admittedly sometimes it can take a while to reach a sustained change. I will never forget the first time I heard my husband say to me, after being asked to do something for me, *"We are a good team, aren't we?"* That was the result of about five years of positive listening on my part! He had no idea why I looked so happy at his comment!

Your opinions, then, define your long-term relationships. They give them the sense and colour and boundaries within which they can operate and flow. If you are madly in love with this amazing woman, then that will influence her and your relationship greatly. If you have little respect for your husband then you will struggle, unless your relationship specifically feeds off this. Your initial opinions provide long-term back up evidence for your prejudices. You will spot all the signs that you are right, you will encourage these and see actions through this filter, and you will not see evidence that speaks otherwise. You are, after all, human.

If you are with me on this point that your opinions form other people, then it follows that people can be who you want them to be - as long as you see your opinions as being up to you. Given the power of your opinion you really need to be careful how you choose it. But can you really choose it? The issue with opinions and judgements about other people is that we relate to them as the "truth", as "right", as soon as we have reached these conclusions. Of course we do - why would you consider your own opinions as wrong? If you were wrong you would think something different, so you must be right instead. It stands to reason. But is any opinion right? Really? A judgement about someone is simply your thought about them at that point in time. You may have undoubted evidence and fact to back up your opinion. But if you look closely at judgements about people they are rarely truly based on facts. "My husband is not caring." It seemed factual. He never offered to help. When asked to help, he refused, forgot or complained. He never asked how I was or how my ailments were. When I told him about something that was wrong he would not follow it up with any comment or question. I am not sure this is totally true, even, but supposing it were, it still does not mean he is "not caring". I made it mean that and it was depressing to realise I had married an uncaring guy. I lived with that for a number of years. Then I realised I was not giving him space to care, and that maybe he did "care" but had no idea how to show it. When I asked him about it, that is exactly what he explained. In fact, he had decided he did not do "caring" or "illness" and literally had no currency, expectation, techniques - nothing. He did not mind me thinking this about him - he already knew this about himself. None of that makes it true, still. I focused on his deeper interest and intention and encouraged a new perspective to emerge through my changing my opinion about him. Changing your opinion requires an openness on your part, a responsibility for it and its potential impact. It takes courage to admit you might be wrong and to try out a new judgement. It takes mature adult thinking and ultimately a "letting go" of previously held beliefs. You may be relieved to hear that my husband is now a very caring partner who is a total stand for the well-being of me and our boys. He likes to be updated on health issues by email, admittedly, and says very little about such matters. What changed was me.

Consider someone who is important to you but with whom you have a challenging relationship. Write down opposite, or privately your judgement of them. Then list all the things they are great at, just to get into a positive perspective. Then clarify the facts about them - did they betray you? Lie to you? Disappoint you? Steal from you? Then be creative, and consider what alternative opinion you could give should you wish to take a new perspective, given the facts. See if you can generate three alternatives and then choose an opinion that will serve you and your relationship in the future.

EXERCISE
How to turn a relationship around

Name	
Opinion	
Three things I like about them	
Facts about them	
Three super-empowering alternative opinions I could have	
Choose a revised opinion to try out	

If you struggle with any of these stages, just ask someone else to help you out. Another perspective might be very interesting and enlightening. At the end of the day, it is your choice whether you hold onto your original opinion, but the invitation is to try out a new and more helpful one. Let me know how you get on.

There are some useful places to stand for access to new perspectives. Look at their commitment, at their strengths and their impact. Look at their contribution and what had you be in relationship with them in the first place. Look at other things that are deeply true and special about that person and it will usually all work out. Look at those you depend on and look at upgrading your opinions everywhere around you. Your whole community and network could literally transform in front of you with little effort on their part and really only a big dose of "letting something go" on your part.

If there is someone critical to you and your life where you find you cannot shift some unhelpful opinions then you may need to look at alternative strategies such as distancing, detaching or managing your boundaries with them differently. Why would you not be surrounded by amazing people you love?

CHAPTER 6

You are the key to changing people's opinions

You may have thought that the key to changing people's opinions is to work on other people, but I am suggesting that the key is you. You cannot make someone change their mind or change their judgements. They are theirs. But you can rely on you. It is you and your behaviour that has caused other people to assess and judge as they have – no one else's - and you are responsible for how you show up.

If you think others think badly, negatively or disempoweringly about you, then the first place to start is to look at what you can change. Some things are easier to shift than others. Making yourself tall when you are small, or male when you are female, for instance, would definitely be in the "hard" category! If you have reviewed your opinion of them and seen nothing lacking then the obvious and most significant next step is to look at altering your intention. This is a profound and key aspect that impacts a relationship dynamic dramatically. If you are trying to impress, for instance, then you could instead aim to have fun and see where that takes you. If you are aiming to have the person like you then you could drop the need or desire for that and look for respect instead.

EXAMPLE

Several years ago I was struggling with one of my team and realised my intention was to turn him around from being a bit anti-authoritarian and disrespectful, and have him respect me as a boss. My 360° data made it very clear that I may have been aiming for this for about 18 months, but I was not getting very far at all. His data stood out amongst all the others' as a broken relationship with no respect, except for how I manage the clients where he described me as "a great schmoozer". I also happened to know what he thought of schmoozing, so you get the picture!

> My strategy was to drop the desire to have him respect me and instead to relate to him as someone totally dedicated to the business with an intention of loving working with him, regardless of his feelings and thoughts for me. Things changed dramatically after that. We had fun. Even others noticed he was respectful and productive in meetings and I shared with him how I had felt, what I had been trying to do and now what my intention was. He relaxed, as if the battle was over - he did not have to prove anything.

Look at what you can accept as "how it is". This is the access to a sense of freedom from the issues that arise out of others' opinions. Thinking something is wrong is horrid and frustrating, especially when you cannot change it. It takes a lot of energy thinking current reality really should be another way. This goes for lots of things, not just others' opinions. It took me a while to get my head around the Brexit result, for instance. I still remember the early hours of the morning when the realisation of the vote came upon people on the news. I did not want it to be true, yet it was. It was upsetting, shocking, as I had had no expectation of this result, and it was worrying. But a day or so later I accepted it had happened and that, somehow, it was OK. Our happiness seems to depend on a grounded and accepting relationship with reality. Pretending you can change someone's opinion of you is simply a recipe for frustration.

Consider that other people's opinions of you, then, are a natural, perfect and logical result from their experience, their observations, their values, their inherited cultural stereotypes, etc. Whether you like them or not, other people are always right to think as they do. The logic automatically works and there is a sense to these things. Even if it seems random, there is a reason and sense to that randomness. Once you have seen how others are right you can start to look at the aspects of their opinion in more detail.

Your main access to changing others' thoughts about you is to change you. You may think this is not fair or right. You might think they are so obviously wrong, surely it is up to them to change? What can you do, when you have done everything you can already? It is easy when facing the effects of stereotypic boundaries (which we all are, as we have ascertained) to feel this way and to take the position of a victim, i.e. "feel(ing) helpless and passive in the face of misfortune or ill-treatment"[21]. It is not your opinion and you cannot control other people, so of course you can feel like you have no power in that matter at all. Easy to feel helpless and hopeless and to focus on how unfair it all is. However, I am suggesting you take an alternative position. You are the one who can manage it, you cannot rely on anyone else. This is an empowering position to take. It gives you your power and makes you responsible for your relationships. It is not true that you are in full control, of course. No one is. But this position allows you to be empowered and encouraged. It gives you the starting blocks for you to play the game that is "managing others' opinions". Without it you are simply a bystander watching it all happen on the field in front of you, about you. It is more fun and more effective to participate.

It may be down to you, but you are not alone. Others can help you. Sponsors and mentors, friends and buddies, can all be useful. Even if in allowing you to explore and enquire about the issues and options. Other senior people in your organisation can be extremely helpful by allowing you access to the senior perspective from a more objective standpoint than perhaps those more directly involved. Consider asking the questions you really want answers to, e.g. *"What do others like X or Y really think of me?"*, *"What do I do that has them think that?"*, *"What do you think I should be doing?"*, *"How can I impress X or Y?"* If your 360° data is showing up some trickiness with those in authority, then an enquiry about how you are relating to those more senior than you is likely to be highly worthwhile. If your 360° points to issues with your peers, then find a friendly colleague to explain things to you. But be careful not to expect anyone else to see through the opinions. Especially if there are profound and stereotypic influences at play, it is likely that literally everyone around you will be guided and influenced the same way. That is the definition of a stereotype - it is "commonly held beliefs", so you may need an external viewpoint or you may need to ensure you make up your own mind.

Why are other people's opinions important? They impact you in every interaction, they form you and impact your ability to influence. If your intention is to be a leader at any level, this is critical. If you know you can influence things you will be empowered and you become the leader of your life, the author of your story. Gaining access to your power and ability to influence other's opinions of you is part of this journey. Powerful and impactful communication is part of the vital toolkit in this area. You need to influence other people. There are ways to impress and relate powerfully to people - ten methods are listed below:

1. **Invite**

   Asking people if they would like to do something, attend something, think something or consider something, etc., is easy and useful. Other people can say yes or no to this. It is but an invitation. It is open but moving things forward. You cannot go wrong with an invitation if you are happy with whatever answer you may receive.

2. **Make an offer**

   Spotting something you can offer to do, buy, get, ask, present, etc., can usefully move a conversation forward. It leads to a trusting and constructive dynamic and encourages others to offer and act as a reciprocal response. You have to remember to fulfil your offer, of course...

3. **Make a promise**

   Promising to do something or get something is useful. It is usual to say "*I'll try,*" or "*I will have a go,*" but much more impressive to say "*I promise to get those figures to you by X time.*" This shows a determination, energy and commitment that less impactful offers do not match. It impresses and reassures. You do then have to manage things if you do not fulfil your promises.

4. Repromise

As soon as you realise you cannot keep a promise the most effective action is to explain and get into communication. It may be OK to repromise or renegotiate, but it is always better to be in communication if circumstances or knowledge have shifted. The earlier the better. More on this later.

5. State your intention

Clarifying explicitly your intention and your commitment is powerful. It allows others to see and be inspired by your aim. If others are not inspired by your goal you then have an opportunity to refine or adjust it so they are. Alternatively, you can drop that intention and turn your energy to something else if you want!

6. Share your perspective

Simply explaining your feelings and thoughts can be very useful in moving things along. Sometimes people need convincing, but this also expands the familiarity and intimacy in the relationship. This can lead to an enhancement of trust and understanding, which can then lead to a more open space of negotiation and agreement.

7. Make a proposal

If action is not clear then formulating a way forward and presenting it as a proposal will generally focus people so that agreement can be reached or the proposed way forward can be adjusted so that alignment is fulfilled.

8. Take on accountability

By offering to take something on, or agreeing to the request to do so, you are putting yourself forward. You will then have a useful access to authority as your accountability will back up further requests you may have.

9. Request

Asking people to do something can be very useful, but you have to be careful using this technique in the more polite cultures, e.g. British, Japanese, as the recipients of requests may consider them as orders, i.e. they may feel they have to say "yes". When there is genuine choice in the matter, then asking someone for something can be a very useful way of moving things forward.

10. Give an instruction

Ordering people to do things at work is a last resort action. It is not guaranteed to work that well, dependant on your culture and norm (and the age and maturity of others). It has a useful place, however, in areas of health and safety, and well-being, where urgency can be critical and life may be at stake.

The main suggestion here is that you powerfully manage others' opinions of you, your personal brand - that you become a personal brand strategist. This requires you to own others' opinions as yours to manage, as a game to engage in, as something worthy of a strategy at all. You can be a victim to others' opinions and relate to your reputation as controlled "over there", somewhere else, but you can relate to it as if you are in charge and have influence. To win at chess you need to know what result you are aiming for and you need to think many moves ahead - not just your own moves, but those of your opponent, and the same principles apply here. Get clear where you really want to get to, identify your key players - your supporters and your opponents - and consider your options. Come up with a Plan A and make sure you have a Plan B in case Plan A does not go the way you want. Your reputation is precious, so think of something you manage really well, e.g. your marriage, your hobby, and take a similar approach.

You are in charge of what you say and do and how you look. You may not always feel fully in charge, but you are, no one else is. You write specific things on social media and in emails. You write books or blogs, or you do not. You take actions, or you do not. You speak up or you keep quiet. You petition or you ignore. You donate or invest, or you do not. You speak from an empowering and supportive intention or from a less constructive position. You wear professional current clothes or you do not. You wear accessories and "badges" that finish off an outfit, e.g. nail varnish, tie, belt, hat, etc., or you do not. You wear make-up at work or you leave it off. You wear bright or unusual colours or ones that make you disappear.

To get us started in looking at potential strategies to change people's minds about you, here are six simple but dramatic ones in summary (with further detail given in the next chapter):

BE YOU	Spot a strategy unique to you that solves an issue you have - it could involve a confession, a job application or the acquisition of something. An example of this arose from a coaching conversation with a senior female leader in a large public organisation. She had had a significant police background and she was very beautiful, manicured and also five feet tall. Through coaching, she discovered that she felt least empowered when she was in her leadership team meetings. After detailed questioning it became clear that the chairs were particularly high in this meeting room and she had the experience of her feet swinging, like they had when she was a girl. Her solution was to arrive early with a small box to put her feet on. Her power was restored.
BE BOLD	Find an opportunity to take the lead and the initiative. Offer to look at the big problem; this may sit outside your remit, but you can see that something needs doing. Find the biggest problem that needs fixing and take some action to sort it out.

BE HONEST	Find opportunities to share and speak the truth about what is happening or what was happened. Look at what you can say that has not already been said. This may expose a totally new space for relating and may serve to clear things up. Look for things you can apologise for inside of an intention of getting things straight so that you can move on.
BEFRIEND	Spot someone in your network you have a positive relationship with and who is committed to the things you are interested in, too. Someone whose reputation is useful to you. Work with them, offer to help them and support them with their goals, and focus on developing the partnership rather than yourself.
BE A NEW LOOK	The investment of a better quality suit or a braver colour can shift you in others' eyes overnight. Dress as you want to be related. If you want to be seen as an important leader, then be sure that you look the part.
BE A NEW YOU	Work out a way to do things differently, even if it is just an experiment to see if things work better this way. I can be a little disorganised and this can be a real problem for some people who do not quite know how to get what they need from me - as clarified by my 360°. I consulted someone very organised and introduced a "Team File" which would allow me to record conversations with everyone in the team more carefully and consistently, and I also introduced one-to-one one-hour meetings with all my direct reports on a fortnightly basis. Since then my team seem more relaxed, knowing there is a place and time for them to raise issues. From my perspective I was always there for them, but my 360° said otherwise.

If you are your brand manager then you would know what your personal website would look like. Not that you have to have one, but to be clear what you would want yours to say, feel and do, can make things very clear - for you and for others around you. What do you want to be known for? What is special about you? What characteristics are truly and deeply you? Be sure only to focus on things that are truly and honestly you, without any effort. It is time to let go of the things that do not suit you that well; just focus on those things that are your favourite glove, the things that fit you snugly and warmly, the things you love and admire. Consider what you would be doing and saying if you were wearing your favourite glove. Learn from the world of corporate and retail brands and consider the bold things you could do to embed and reinforce your brand. Presence your key stories and significant facts in your history, wear the right clothes for your brand, and then look to manage the listening of other people on an ongoing, everyday basis. Set up feedback loops to ensure you are getting it right. This is a job that applies to every conversation with everyone.

CHAPTER 7

Strategies to change opinions

PART 1 - Change how you relate to their opinions

You have just read the summary suggestions as to how to manage your brand, but if you really seriously want to deal with a tricky opinion from an individual or a group then this chapter will outline three different strategies in detail. Each of these can transform this issue for you. I have seen all of them work via my own experience and in that of my coachees.

These powerful strategies are presented starting with the easiest (or at least the one requiring the least action) and ending with what many might consider to be the hardest - the one where you change. There are three different overall approaches - first how to work better with the opinions that others have about you, second how to change yourself so the opinions can shift and third, how to change your context so that you and others' opinions are less destructive. Please consider all of these before choosing which will work best for you. Your ideal may well be a combination of a few of these so the suggestion is to read them all and then decide. You will create the ideal strategy for yourself when you have immersed yourself in these options, so just enjoy the experience in the meantime.

These strategies all work and they all require focused intention to do so. Some will strike you as easier or more attractive than others... let me hear your stories by sharing on my website[22]. We start with where it is easiest to control - with you.

STRATEGY 1
Be you

This is easy and hard all at the same time. It is easy to appreciate others' opinions if they are good ones, but it may seem to you impossible to even like or just understand those that work against you. It is as easy as letting go of a pen and as hard as dropping that grudge that you have lived with forever. This is the territory of acceptance, of reaching understanding of "*That is how it is*". This is what happens when you end up sighing and suggesting "*Well, it's done now*". But it is not just moving on and looking forwards, it is also about forgiving with compassion and acceptance. It is reaching a point where it truly is "OK" the way that it was. It is choosing to see the situation as perfect, with nothing being wrong about it. Everything was in order and just fine. Just imagine these sentiments - they leave you relaxed and content, possibly sanguine, definitely wise. This is a mature response where there is no room for childish reactions and emotional vendettas. It is a loving and peaceful space. It is a place for laughter and hilarity. You know you are in this space if you can truly and happily laugh about it.

So, how do you reach this position? There are a number of stages in this process:

* **STEP 1 - Seeing that you are the one who is suffering**

  While you focus on how wrong the others are, you are the one who is experiencing frustration and stress. You are upset with their opinions. They are fine with their opinions just the way they are (otherwise they would shift them). In fact, it is more than this. The key here is to see that you are gaining something from having an issue with their opinions in the first place. You may think this is bonkers. Of course you do not get anything out of it! *"It's horrid!"* you may say. But look again. There is something you are getting out of it. It might be simply that you get to be right while they are wrong, or it could be that it proves a fear or insecurity you have about yourself. *"I always knew I wasn't good enough, here's proof."* It could be that you get to dominate or control people or a situation, or simply that it justifies some behaviour or experience in the past - or something you are planning in the future. The basic assumption is that if you are holding onto something that negatively impacts you, you are definitely getting something out of it. You are too committed to survival to continue hurting yourself with no gain. Unless "self-harm" is the key aim you want to reinforce, of course. You can see the circularity of the argument.

- ## STEP 2 - Accepting the opinions are fair and legitimate

This simply means that you let go of any arguments or justifications that prove them otherwise. Your rationalisation and defensive arguments disappear into the background and you focus instead on seeing how logical and valid their opinions truly are. You see how they could not have reached any other opinion. It is an obvious, natural position that they find themselves in that place. This requires you to really get that everyone's opinions are formed logically and reasonably as a result of their beliefs and experience, their genetic inheritance, their cultural background and origins, etc. It always makes sense.

Our brains do not tolerate things that do not make sense, even if the facts are false, the interpretations may not be valid, the intelligence may be lacking. There is still a logic to everyone's processing - even if the logic is illogical. All there is to do then is to make that assumption, i.e. other people think this and it is logical and reasonable that they do, and then you can start to see and understand the dynamic and perspective better.

- ## STEP 3 - Being OK with their position

You can now accept their opinions as valid, but is it really OK? Again there is an opinion of yours entering the process. Why would it not be OK? You may understand where their opinion has come from and have an opinion yourself about them and about their position. You may have quite a negative opinion about them, in fact! This is a natural and easy reaction to see and feel. You get they do not respect you, so you respond by not respecting them. Quite frankly, why would you do otherwise? Such negative reciprocity may be natural, but it is not ideal.

- ## STEP 4 - Being OK with life being this way

Being OK with life being this way. You can rightfully think that things should be different from how they are, but this does not get you very far. You can be angry and you can campaign, but those leaders who make things different can be seen to manage their emotions with fortitude and peaceful wisdom. They accept and love how it is at the same time as being committed to things being different. This is maturity and something for most of us to aim for, but well worth looking in this direction. If you are really OK with how it is, then you can freely and powerfully choose how you want to relate to it and whether you want to act in relation to it.

EXAMPLE

An experienced CEO of a local council was frustrated. She had run a successful council for five years but she still did not seem to have all the managers' respect. She had realised there were puzzling blocks in her ability to be an effective leader a while back but her 360° report showed her this lack of positive respect in glorious technicolour. She was upset and angry at first. None of these ratings and comments made much sense. But, after we had pulled them apart, she could see that some individuals were determined to see her in a certain way. She was seen as weak, but when she was strong she was criticised and undermined. In terms of professional expertise her leadership was working, in terms of people management she was in a bind.

It took some processing and expressing of emotion to come to a point where she could relate to these opinions as OK, as valid and legitimate. It helped to see the cultural norms which might have been playing out. There was a bigger macho-centred value set hidden within individual opinions. Seeing herself as one within generations and centuries of gender norming allowed her let go of seeing the opinions as personal to her. She started to smile again and accepted her situation as it was. In terms of moving forward she then saw she had options.

She could face this battle head-on or take a more strategic long term approach. She started to review her career plan differently and to relax into her accountabilities. After having been highly stressed and exhausted, she then had a great year, after which she moved to be CEO of a charitable organisation that totally inspired her.

STRATEGY 2
Be bold

You may be very clear that an opinion is wrong and think that all you need to do is to challenge the logic or the facts behind it and that will be that. If only it were that easy! Feel free to try, but unfortunately you might find that it is harder to shift someone's position than this. As covered earlier, it is useful to remember that everyone's opinions are justifiably and logically made, given who they are, their values, their intentions and their perspective. Imagine someone trying to change your opinion on something or someone? Just the idea of it can lead you to think and feel a "*just you try*" sensation of resistance. People do not generally like being persuaded. It can easily feel like pressure and, even if the argument is totally compelling, they can end up feeling pushed into it and a sense of being "bullied", i.e. feeling "intimidated by those who are stronger"[23]. This can occur especially easily if someone is very skilful at inspiring and "wooing". The dynamic is not fruitful and an attempt to change their mind can result in more detachment and polarisation of views. You could end up with them taking an even more fixed and extreme view than they held in the first place!

So should you not even try? Not necessarily. However, you should only try with this risk in mind. You are best to approach this strategy by looking at how you might carefully and skilfully change their mind. There are a number of different ways:

- **Option 1**

  Use someone else to change their mind by finding a supporter who could go to work on your behalf.

- **Option 2**

  Find or create a new circumstance or fact that you can bring into the mix. This will then give them a legitimate excuse to change their mind.

- **Option 3**

  Focus on something bigger than their opinion of you and get them on board with this new bigger thing. This will drive a new approach and may allow their opinion of you to disappear and be redundant in the face of this larger context.

- **Option 4**

  Face them with courage and apologise for how you have been - fully owning that their opinions were spot on. Clarify your newly revised intentions and prove through action that your new efforts are aligned. Speak and show how different you are now. Thank them for being the catalyst to this new and useful development.

- **Option 5**

  Questioning and exploring with them what you would need to do differently could allow you to move forward, as long as you are genuine in your enquiry. "*What can I do to show you I am...?*" The advantage of this conversation is that it allows them to express themselves in a constructive fashion. They may drop the issue through this conversation, but if they do not then you are likely to discover more about what they really think, the source of their views and the impact it might be having on them. This may equip you to handle things differently and lead to your resolving the issue another way.

- **Option 6**

   Work to prove them wrong, ensure you are building the "brownie points" with them and when your good work is really clear, just gently ask them, "*Do you trust me now?*" (or whatever the pertinent issue is). In the moment they may let go of their previous issue. It is a commitment choice in the moment, a letting go of the pen, and it could be the end of the issue.

There are other options, no doubt, but you can see that these are quite dramatic initiatives. They require effort and courage on your part and then you cannot guarantee that the other party will oblige as you want them to. You have to be prepared that other people can be so committed to being right about their opinions that any logical, reasonable action on your part simply makes them turn to their point of view more strongly, just because. Sometimes these can work, however.

EXAMPLE

An investment banker had been recently promoted to manage a team across Geneva and London. He was clearly a brilliant professional, and a master in his field and with his clients. His new direct reports told a different story, however. His 360 showed up how some of his team considered him unfocused and unclear. They were not getting what they needed from him and were not impressed. After initial surprise and puzzlement, he could see that these opinions seem to come from those he considered not quite up to their jobs.

His initial reaction was to try to fix this and give more direction, etc., but instead he coached and challenged them over the next six months and looked to identify someone in his team to help him manage his large team as his workload was unreasonably demanding. Some ended up leaving his team and others came good, but overall these negative opinions were accepted and then challenged in a constructive manner.

STRATEGY 3
Show up the bias

One of the factors impacting you and forming others' opinions could be stereotypic bias - this is very likely, actually, as already described. In fact, if there is a situation you are struggling with, it might be interesting to assume there is some bias and to consider what it might be. Just review the full list of possible areas of bias and you might spot something. But you don't even have to identify quite where the bias is coming from or on what basis, to work with it. You just have to consider that there might be a factor or theme larger than yourself influencing thinking, something getting in your way that is not personal to you and not in your control.

The first step in this strategy is to spot it and then to accept it as it is. It is essential to ensure you do not feel angry or upset about this bias. I realise this is a tall order when we are talking about something that might appear to be unjust and unfair, but it is worth looking at how you can get yourself feeling OK about it. Biases exist for good and healthy reasons and emerge through generations of humanity and survival. They work to a point, otherwise they would not exist as they do. You may simply be a victim of them where others are not. If you can take the broad and historical view then you might manage.

This strategy is to show up the bias without judgement and without disempowering other people. There are four ways to do this:

1. Plan for bias

Assume you will have bias facing you and impacting you adversely, and work out a way that will still allow you what you need. This may mean that you compensate by bringing other people in or that you assign accountabilities appropriately. This may feel like you are pandering and giving in to the bias to some extent, so you may want to take on one of the other options at the same time.

EXAMPLE

I felt I was facing significant bias as a woman in charge of a commercial business and felt others were not taking my views on business strategy seriously; they were not listening to me as an authority. After ten years of managing a successful business in a tough market this felt disempowering and deeply frustrating.

After a few years of taking it personally and then trying other strategies, I decided the success of my business was at stake and was more critical than my position on the matter. I appointed a male no.2 to support me, to be my strong voice of business authority. However, this only really worked while this individual could accept that he reported to me.

After six months my first choice no.2 refused to accept my authority, which was galling in itself, but it deeply undermined my confidence and authority with my team, too, so needed urgent exit. I found a great alternative with a different contractual relationship and a very different intention to empower me as the owner, which worked brilliantly.

2. Unhook their biased "cogs"

You need to be ready and poised to do this as it best happens in the moment. This is highly effective in a conversation, though it may not have your desired long-term impact. How this works is to notice a judgement occur and to respond by accurately providing a mirror for this judgement, i.e. describing exactly what you have seen, with no judgement or issue, just like an observation. You then verbalise this judgement in a neutral fashion and it has a magical effect. The biased person tends to be stopped in their tracks and will normally rethink the conversation. They may not be conscious of this "unhooking", but you can see it.

EXAMPLE

I was in a meeting with my accountant of twelve years and a male colleague and noticed that my suggestions and observations were being a little ignored. My male colleague was getting more attention and respect, although he had less experience and knowledge of my business and my market, and of running a business generally.

With my next suggestion I started with, "*Well, of course, I am no authority on business, but...*" and gave my idea. I saw my accountant agree with me at first. i.e. that I indeed was no authority, but then I saw him double-take and say. "*No, well...*" and he looked at me afresh, as if maybe I did know about my business after all. He then seemed to hear my idea properly - as if my reflecting what was in his unconscious brain had had it disappear for a moment and allowed him to listen without bias. Sneaky but effective.

3. Paint an alternative scenario

Changing the type reference to make a very clear and powerful point. This method is dramatic and poignant - one to be saved up for critical issues and possibly as last resort. If you are really clear that a stereotyping is occurring unhelpfully then pick your time and place carefully to describe an alternative scenario to this person where the types involved in their bias are swapped around. An extension of this strategy is also to change your type temporarily to make a point or to experience the reverse impact. An example of this was quoted widely in the media recently when two people doing the same job, but who were different genders, swapped their email signatures [24] with dramatic effects - accidentally at first and then deliberately for two weeks to explore this shocking experience. The man described work as very tough as "Nicole" and Nicole found her new identity as "Martin" meant things became extremely easy!

EXAMPLE

I was struggling with my mother thinking that it was OK that my brother should demand the same pay as me, even though it was my business, I was MD, I was fourteen years older and more experienced than he was. This was clearly very tricky and I did not want to destroy family relations, but logical argument had got me nowhere.

I picked my time and asked my mother to imagine that my daughter (who happens to be rather conveniently near to fourteen years younger than my brother) had joined my brother's business, had learnt lots from him as MD and, after five years, had demanded to be paid the same as him. I asked my mother what she would think if that happened and she started to say how ridiculous that was! She stopped mid-sentence and never mentioned the issue with my brother again!

You may be glad to hear that, with this slightly unhelpful influence calming, I was soon able to propose a creative deal with my brother which left family relations intact.

4. Calling it out

Speaking about the issue explicitly and assertively. This is straightforward and courageous at the same time. Speaking explicitly about something that is unconscious and largely unspoken takes guts. The problem with this strategy is that others may still respond by attempting to defend and justify their position and it can look like an excuse. This technique involves clarifying that you are indeed "blond" or "short" or whatever it is that you think is getting in the way. The best way of delivering this is to name the truth of who you are without reference to a qualification.

EXAMPLE

An experienced head of HR of a global financial company had a new CEO. She was inspired by this new guy but was struggling with his view of her as being "non-commercial". She brought this issue to a coaching session and it was clear to her that it did not seem to make any difference how commercially she talked or how focused on the bottom line her actions were, he seemed to be determined to see her this way. It meant he did not get the value of her input and her ideas and she felt like she was justifying herself all the time. She was using the FD to back her up, which had been quite effective, but she was getting tired of working around this issue. She started to *"call it out"*. She would start her briefings with something along the lines of: *"I would normally suggest we do X and Y, but, if I am focused on a commercial way forward, I would suggest Z."*

> The CEO did not have to put in his "non-commercial" angle any more as she was doing it for him so, instead he could focus on the ideas themselves and they could have a more productive conversation.

None of these options are guaranteed with success in terms of changing people's mind re the bias, but they are all empowering to you and can lead to a manageable and workable way forward for you and those around you. With these approaches, you can move forward at the same time as not criticising other people. You are exposing something that may need updating.

At the same time, bringing a stereotype into consciousness without forcing people into an avoidance or resistance response is potentially the most powerful thing you can do to change the stereotype for the future. The more this happens, the more fluid prejudice may become.

CHAPTER 8

Strategies to change opinions

PART 2 - Change yourself

This is perhaps the obvious way forward, but changing yourself is not always so easy or even what you want to do. In addition to this, it may not work. You may be totally different but the original judgements of you may remain fixed as it takes more than new evidence to rewire someone else's brain about you. Nevertheless, there is an obvious place for these options, so they are well worth consideration.

STRATEGY 4
Do exactly what they ask

If there is something others do not like about you then, rather than being frustrated, upset or just bored, you could look at this feedback as a request for something. People are asking for something from you. They may be asking you to be more structured, to be more engaging or to be more empathic. You can see this as indicators of their needs rather than signs of your incompetence. You can then decide whether you want to consider responding to their requests and how you want to respond. If you are being asked to fix something, you could very simply aim to do exactly this. You could even ask for their help.

Feedback is usually deemed a good thing at work these days. It allows you to see your blind spots and reinforces those behaviours people appreciate. In theory, feedback allows you to see what others do not like as well. You can see feedback as a gift. You get given it even if sometimes you do not even ask for it or want it - a bit like the Christmas gift mentioned earlier. It can be unsolicited and unwanted, or it can be very much desired. Either way, you may not like it. This strategy, though, is about looking at it, trying on that you can deliver exactly what is being asked of you and getting on with it quite happily. The results will be what they will be.

I am generally responsive and flexible with people, which has the downside of being less structured, organised and rigid than some can cope with, as noted already. Can I take actions to be more organised? Yes, indeed I can, not for me but for others. My PA is part of my answer and seems to leave people with the control and certainty they want. They now have the new issue of having to negotiate their way to me via a tough PA...

As you can see this strategy does not require you to totally change your personality, but it does require you to listen and acknowledge others' needs and to get committed to delivering something different. That requires a change of heart and new actions on your part. It is not passive and is not for those with pride beyond humility, but it will be received very positively. If you get it right, then you will get brownie points from other people. Their view or complaint about you will then dissipate and become less impactful, rather than totally disappear.

An example of this came up in a 360° feedback with a highly visible and well-known head of a public organisation. He was highly respected by all of his reviewers, but there were specific aspects that did not work for people. There was a consistent message, and this message was taken very seriously by this CEO. He totally agreed with the issue, but had not seen until now quite how hard it was for others to handle this weakness. He had a real lack of interest in general, operational practicalities, but he thought he had that handled with the team around him. His 360 made it clear there was more to do, however, and the impact on him and his ability to deliver his next big plans for the organisation were at stake. As this project was a huge investment and highly visible internationally, he took this insight seriously and set to put more provision and resource in place to ensure colleagues and the whole organisation had what they needed. He appointed a more senior COO and things started to feel smoother.

The critical thing with this strategy is to remember that it is not an overnight fix, but there needs to be a continual process of checking and monitoring to ensure needs and expectations are being fulfilled. Once you have the commitment to deliver what others need of you, though, this will become easy.

STRATEGY 5
Share and share again

If you carry on having the exact same conversations that you have always had, then you will get the same results you have always got. Simply saying something new and fresh will make a difference. Expressing yourself is an empowering thing to do regardless of what you say, but if you say some things with the intention to clarify, move things forward and help a situation, then it will likely do exactly that. There is, however, always a good reason why you have not said this stuff already - in your head, anyway. It may not "feel right" or you may think there is something to risk in saying those things. That may be true. Relationships can indeed be sensitive and fragile things, but usually it is the case that a constructive, helpful intention will normally help move things forward rather than destroy. If a relationship cannot take you expressing yourself with considered honesty then perhaps there is something false or broken in the very foundations of that relationship already? Maybe it is not worth tending if it cannot take a little more truth? These are important and bold things to consider.

How come sharing is even a good idea? The total opposite can be argued - when is honest sharing ever not a good idea? The important issue here is to look at what it is you might want to share. If it includes your negative opinion and critical judgement of others then you should stop. This is not for sharing; instead you should look at how you can shift from this position. Sharing vile opinion will destroy and damn. If your sharing includes your experience and the consequences of others' behaviour then this is usually very useful. Get super clear exactly what your experience is and what prompts it and make sure you are not emotionally charged about this before describing it. This is a conversation which may be truly heard and may shift the dynamic and the relationship forever. Talk more explicitly about your intentions and your commitments. This is the time to consider communicating powerfully by referring to the methods listed earlier. This is about showing your vulnerability and your true feelings and motives. It is about others understanding you better. It is about sharing intimacy and thereby creating familiarity and trust. It is about positioning yourself as someone with empowering intention who is not willing to have certain things going on around them. You are managing your boundaries and opening yourself up at the same time. If you speak where you have not spoken before, then you will be creating a new future and a new realm for others to be within and you will end up relating to yourself more powerfully, as others will, too.

Sharing can only happen when "issues" you may have, have been put into the background. Otherwise it is not sharing but it is complaining. Complaining leaves the other person to deal with, manage, justify, defend, walk away or simply listen. Sharing requires you to take full responsibility for your own experience and actions, for your previous tolerance and actions, for your previous lack of communications, for your emotional responses to someone else. Once you have done this there literally may be nothing left to say, or there may be much to discuss.

Always check your purpose in talking, check it with a buddy who does not easily go along with your complaints and grumbles, someone who challenges how you relate to things. Be careful not to confuse "sharing" with "righteous indignation" and then be courageous and share with transformation in mind.

STRATEGY 6
Confess your real intention

What is really going on with you? Often when there are opinions around that are not positive, there are misunderstood and/or misaligned intentions. Things can be cleared up by speaking out and stating explicitly what it is you are wanting or aiming to achieve. This does not mean other people will necessarily like it or comply simply with your requests, but it does mean that it makes things clearer for you and for them. This can shift the dynamic of the relationship and can enable more to be said and thereby resolved. Confessing your real intention can expose the truth in a transformational way. If nothing else, it gives you a chance to feel like you have been fully self-expressed. If others want to think what they want to think, it is up to them... you have given it your best shot. The critical follow-up to your restating and insistence re your intention is to position the logical reason and connections so others get the truth of this intention, then the actions and consequences of this need to follow with a vigorous pointing back to your stated intention. You have to make it dead simple, logical and obvious.

Critical also to this strategy, however, is for you to realise that all of this will not automatically change people's minds. You will be more effective here if you are OK with them getting it and also with them not getting it at all. If you can accept that they will make up their own minds (and probably already have) and that whatever you do and say will make no difference, then you will enjoy the attempt to clarify things. This will ultimately be more persuasive, though still, of course, not guaranteed. You can count on people being dogmatic and determined and very "right" about their viewpoints, which automatically means any opposing or differing view will be "wrong".

EXAMPLE

Towards the end of a restructure, a young head of HR was struggling to come to agreement with her boss, the COO, regarding her job grade. She realised that her logical arguments and evidence were falling on deaf ears and somehow he had decided she should not be at the higher grade. The COO was unusually anti-status and did not engage fully in any conversation about grades and titles, etc., but in this case it was down to him. Seeing the need for a change of tack, she was inspired to share her real desire.

She looked at the true reason for her request. The terms at the new grade included a bigger notice period and, with potential redundancies coming, this was the key thing she wanted. She skipped the prologue and said, *"I'm worried about the coming redundancies and would feel much more comfortable with the higher notice period - I don't really care about the grade per se."* This honesty got the desired upgrade with ease and speed.

STRATEGY 7
Clear up disappointments

If a relationship is not free and easy with totally understood agreements and a positive way of relating then a good place to start is to check where the disappointments are. Disappointments arise when hopes and expectations are unfulfilled. They arise when someone thinks you should be being some particular way or doing some particular thing. They may have told you or asked you to do certain things, but they may not have done. They may simply have expected you to anyway. These are the really nasty potholes to stumble into! They are not necessarily of your making directly, but impact you hugely and it is your job to drag them out into the open to be unconcealed and cleared up. You may be wondering what this has got to do with changing someone's opinion of you; the point is that people's views and opinions are not based on a pure logical analysis of your skills and potential, but instead will be affected by people's experience of you.

The issue is that disappointment and some key critical issues can affect your reputation so seriously and so negatively that they can mask any other possible thoughts. Think about someone you have heard about in the news recently who has been accused of some major wrongdoing. This fact is likely to be the key focus of your attention, not any other facts or previously held opinions about their finer qualities. Reputations are made and broken on this basis. It is as if there is a foundation of ethics or integrity that has to be in place before more sophisticated assessment can even take place. Our brains are very much wired to focus on the negative and this phenomenon is a powerful mechanism by which our societies manage themselves. We make it very clear that there are rules by which you have to live to be fully accepted and heard. At the end of the day, it is our voices that impact us and the conversations that we have and the listening is seriously and critically influenced by whether the audience considers us as fulfilling our word.

A 360° feedback report can indicate that this is the strategy to use. One sign is having many low ratings, e.g. "1"s (=poor) or "2"s (=fair) in a 5-point rating scale, and/or when there are specific low ratings on behavioural statements that refer to "fairness", "honesty", "transparency", "fulfilling promises", "ethical", etc. In addition, this may be a good strategy when there are open comments referring to a lack of consistency, changing mind, saying one thing and doing another, not walking the talk. There may not be many signs, but even a few mean this is worth serious attention. In this respect, people rarely give you a second chance.

They know what you are like and what you can do and it is going to take something significant to change their mind. As far as they are concerned there is nothing to fix and no consequences for them. You just are this way. The impact is on you and it is for you to act. Here are some areas to look at:

1. Is it an issue of honesty?

This is tricky stuff but when others think you are not quite telling the truth, the dynamic can shift immediately and the relationship can start to head in a negative direction. Lying can happen with the best intention and it can happen accidentally, or carelessly. Either way, it can be spotted. Discrepancies can be picked up at later times without your being aware. And "shades of the truth" can be the result of a different perspective and different ways of interpreting the same thing. You can count on people noticing such things and also on them not necessarily telling you what they have noticed. You will be in the dark and there will be no trial or jury and no opportunity to defend yourself!

RESOLUTION

Attempt to tease out the detailed perspective from others if you are not clear what inconsistencies have occurred. Once you are aware, then you are best coming clean and confessing to where you have lied or misled people. Explaining why and apologising, being clear that you are committed to speaking the truth in the future. It takes serious sincerity and courage to speak in this way. There is no guarantee you will be forgiven, but you may get a second chance.

2.   Have you been "unfair"?

Your values are likely to be slightly, if not significantly, different from others' values. The particular cocktail of things you hold as important is specific to you, but others may not understand or appreciate that and will judge you on your actions against their own value set and their own understanding of the facts. Many people have a strong sense of equity and a need for fairness and it is easy for misunderstandings to occur that lead people to consider actions as unfair. This sense of unfairness then translates to an opinion of you that will impact you significantly - in terms of trust or believing that you are not "a good manager" or simply in terms of your opinion of them not being known to be positive. If you believe that someone is not on your side then you will naturally be a little cautious and potentially defensive. It is not an empowering foundation for a working relationship.

RESOLUTION

This is a tricky one to resolve unless you hear their case and change position, and even then, they may still think you have been unfair and still maintain a degree of issue with you. The best approach is to explain your thinking and state very clearly your intention and your commitment, including that of being fair. There may then be openness to seeing you differently but you need to be prepared that they may maintain their position. If that is the case, you may want to look out for obvious examples to pointedly prove your point and use someone else to influence them. Unfortunately, this is a case of the more you defend and justify your position, the less you may be heard.

3. **Did you change your mind?**

Circumstances change or you learn something fresh and decide to change your course of action. This is perfectly reasonable but beware, as sometimes others may see this as inconsistent and flaky. They may later consider that your word cannot be counted on. They would be right, of course, but that is not the point. This is natural immersive agility in a fast-changing world which, when combined with committed leadership and promises, can be tricky to handle. Some relationships around you will understand exactly how you are managing things and evolving your ideas but not everyone will, so be prepared for negative opinion from such flexibility.

RESOLUTION

The best approach is to share with all the key people how your thinking is evolving, having it be the thinking of the group and not just you. Acknowledging the detail and signposting pivots in the journey all help others understand the process, but perhaps the most critical thing is to be really clear what your long-term and overarching commitment is. Find the goal you are totally and 100% committed to achieving, the thing you will not waiver from. It might be "the £1 million" or "beat the competition" or to "attract 100 customers a day", where the goal maintains but the "how" might shift. Some people will only be impressed if you keep to your goal, so find a goal to keep.

4. Did you break your promise?

If you said you would deliver this week then the following Monday morning is late. If you said you would get twenty people on a course, then eighteen is short. If you said you would write a two-page summary, then a ten-page one is too long. There are many ways to promise and there are many other ways to break it. First thing to note is that you do not need to use the word "promise" to leave people with that sense of commitment, so holding back on using that word makes no real difference, apart from making you sound weaker.

Some think you should never "promise" as you cannot be sure you can deliver, ever. That is true, of course. Things happen - climatic disasters, unexpected medical and family emergencies, failures in support, technical breakdowns, lack of inspiration, unforeseen circumstances, etc. You do not fully control your world, so how can you really promise?

You can promise if you have the absolute and full intention to deliver it and work 100% to achieve it. Then you might still fail. Your reputation will be weakened if you break your promise. Your word will be seen less powerfully and you will be trusted less often. But this opinion is seen in the light of your history with this person and the strength of your current starting point. It is as if you have "integrity" points. You simply have to continually work hard to keep the brownie point jar filled above a reasonable level. The acceptable threshold will vary for each person and those closest to you will normally be the most forgiving.

RESOLUTION

If there is a promise you are worried about, get into communication about it as soon as you know it is likely to be a problem - ideally as soon as the circumstances have changed or you realise something is demanding more than you expected. Getting good at this is critical when you are keeping many different priority "balls" up in the air at a time. Acknowledge that you realise the deadline was X or the goal was Y and describe your full-on actions and what has changed since you agreed to this promise. Ideally this is a conversation which will be helpful and lead to you recreating the project or task so that it works again. Sometimes it can end up being in better shape than in the beginning! Taking responsibility and apologising is a critical part of this conversation, as is a restating of your commitment and interest in delivering something. Dealing with a broken promise powerfully and renegotiating can end up being more impressive than simply achieving the original goal, as it takes courage and humility.

5. Did you forget?

This one gets me all the time!? And probably even more than I know! We humans do have a habit of saying things then misremembering what was said, or simply forgetting it altogether. The lack of accuracy of the witness' evidence can be shocking, so this is a common and ordinary phenomenon. If you are good at remembering detailed dates and promises then this won't be such an issue for you, but if you are not, then you will need a range of structures and help to support you manage a heavy schedule. I personally have a PA, a detailed diary with every hour accounted for with meetings or tasks, a notebook in date order with all client promises written in and circled (with a noticeable big circle!) and I also have team members tasked to remind me of critical stuff I might forget. In addition to this, I ask people to email my PA if I promise something when I can't write things down, e.g. when on the move. And still things get missed, I am sure. This is in the same territory as breaking a promise but usually has a lesser level of significance; however, again, it is as if you have a pot of brownie points with each relationship and you do have to work to replenish them if you have lost too many.

RESOLUTION

Getting into communication as soon as you realise you have forgotten something is critical, but unfortunately this one can disappear into forgotten nothingness for obvious reasons... so it is worth checking with key people "*Is there anything I need to do?*" and certainly worth checking specifically with individuals if you sense that there is something negative in the relationship that was not there before. Unfortunately, again, they may not let you know. Tricky territory!

6. Did you do something wrong, but you have no idea what?

This one is a real challenge. You can tell someone is upset with you or not as close or trusting as they were, and you cannot tell what has happened. If they are not saying, then it is likely to be difficult to have them open up, but you can try. The fact is that other people have sensitivities, needs and expectations which may be unexpected and which may vary and change over time. It is not reasonable to expect to be able to satisfy everyone all the time without some "accidental" issues. So the important thing to do is to not take it personally yourself, but do take action to resolve it as it is affecting you. It is probably affecting them but, if you have noticed they are being different with you (and not in a good way), then it is impacting you.

RESOLUTION

First you want to reflect on what has happened and when the relationship shifted. Did you do something? Not do something? Did something happen? Or not happen? If you can track it back to a time or occasion, then you can perhaps then work out a hypothesis about what happened and you can plan to put it right, apologise for doing wrong or get it cleared up. If you have no idea when or what, though, you can simply ask someone "*Have I done something that I shouldn't have done?*" with a genuine request for exposure and sharing. They may or may not divulge. If not, you can check with someone else who might have observed something. The tertiary step is to be direct but open, by asking something like "*I feel I have let you down somehow, how can I make it up to you?*" or "*What can I do to get my colleague back?*" You might find that such questioning, in being bold and showing your vulnerability, will shift the relationship to a more positive place, even though you may not ever get a straight or clear answer about what you have actually done or said; something you may simply have to live with.

7. Did you misunderstand things?

Things can go horribly wrong if you misunderstand a situation and you will not realise it until it happens. It will then usually take a while for you to work out that your understanding is wrong and another perspective is more accurate. You will likely want to keep hold of being "right" for as long as possible! Wherever there is a difference of opinion there will be defensiveness and justification and attempts to persuade the other parties to the alternative way of thinking, so it is best to try to unpick this as soon and as easily as possible.

RESOLUTION

Clarifying that you are seeing a situation a different way from others is a great first step, as is stating your intention to explore and understand things better. Then you need to listen hard to what others are saying and work to clarify what is agreed between you. If there are insignificant areas you disagree on you can note them, but let them go. If you disagree on big ones then you can explore together what might prove it one way or another. Sometimes this can lead to a split in direction, to differences in opinion and strategies; this is the stuff of boardroom dramas, so be careful how you tread. Consider getting input from expert outsiders, your accountant, your coach or mentor, a successful businessman, etc. You can always put a time trial in place, e.g. *"If we do X for three months and I am right about this, then we should get Y result - are you prepared to do that?"*

8. Did you betray someone?

Betrayal is not discussed as openly in business as it could be, but 360° feedback reports can show this up. Betrayal, defined as *"failing to be loyal, often by doing something harmful"*,[25] occurs when someone has acted or spoken with significant negative consequences for someone else. It might be intentional or accidental, but it is always horrible. You know when you have been betrayed. It feels like the floor has been taken away; it leaves you feeling slightly sick and usually very upset or angry. The betrayer may not know the extent of the consequences, but they will know they have done something that hurts. This is part of the betrayal - a conscious, harmful act. You may not know who and how you have betrayed, but you will normally know you have hurt someone, so consider that all those "hurts" could be considered a betrayal and may need clearing up.

RESOLUTION

Here is the bad news - there is little you can do here! You can apologise for hurting them and you can acknowledge what you did and explain why you did it, but you may not be forgiven. You may not even be able to say any of these things as communications often break down fully at this point, for at least a period of time, anyhow. The first thing to do is to accept there is a rift in the relationship that may never be mended. You might, if you work at it, get to a position where you relate around this rift - like you carry on after a broken bone is mended. Your broken rib will never be quite the same as it was, but you can still function. This depends on the commitment and openness of both parties. Resolution is not in the hands of just you.

There are other ways you can disappoint people - through simple miscommunication, through overly abrupt or energetic delivery, through being hopeless, careless, simply by being you, sometimes. There are enough listed above to give you a feel, but the general approach is to notice if something is "off" with an important relationship and to look actively at what you might have done or not done to have caused it. And to accept that you are only human in needing to clear up your own mess. Nothing is wrong, even when it feels like stuff is going totally wrong.

STRATEGY 8
Prove the new you

Other people want you to change. A straightforward strategy, therefore, is to change exactly as requested and to prove it to them! You may have been resisting this for a number of very good reasons. It may seem impossible to change. It seem unreasonable, too. But at a certain point you may choose this path. Taking on this desire may seem like the tough thing to do, but actually it is just the start. Critical to this strategy is ensuring that the important people notice that it has happened.

So consider what evidence would fit the new you. It is worth looking at what you might do or say that would fit the you that you need to be:

> *What conversations would you be having?*
> *What job would you apply for?*
> *What extra responsibilities might you take on?*
> *What new meeting would you call?*
> *What new projects would you contribute to?*
> *What new sale would you go for?*
> *What new make-up or haircut or colour would you try?*
> *What would your desk look like?*

> *What would your office look like?*
> *What would your car look like?*
> *What new qualification would you go for?*
> *What new look would you try?*
> *What new statement would you make?*
> *What new action would you take?*
> *What new structure would you try at work? At home?*

There are many examples I can give you as I reckon this might be my favourite strategy! I was looking for new responsibilities in HR in my twenties, but I was young for my position and I could tell that my senior colleagues did not quite understand what I was prepared and happy to take on. Having realised this, I started wearing a full formal dress suit (yes, trousers were actually banned!) whereas I was previously wearing smart, but not that smart. Dress as you want to be seen, not as who you simply are.

When I wanted to assert my authority I called a regular one-to-one every fortnight and made sure to keep this schedule, taking notes and raising things more formally and thoroughly than I had done before. In addition to this, I organised for an office move and an arrangement where I had my own office, rather than being one of a team of fourteen in open-plan. This had significant impact as, every day, everyone in the team had to enter my office to talk to me. I then had to put things in place to ensure I was approachable and listening, but a stamp of authority was achieved. A year later I did not need this anymore, but instead found a new open-plan office where I could be part of the team as well as the boss.

These physical aspects of your life are critical. They impact you and others at an unconscious level. They are part of your personal brand. They have you sit tall or walk with authority. You (and more importantly, others), do not have to think about what they think, they simply get you the way the structure and conditions allow them to. Use this to your advantage and with full consciousness.

So, first get clear what you could change to back up the newly revised you. Remember that visible things will make great impact but also that altering your "being", i.e. your attitude and/or your intention, can also be extremely impactful. If you have been sullenly tolerating things that don't work for ages but then take on being more self-expressed and powerful, you will start to speak up. Implement a change with joy and eagerness, perhaps even a sense of wonder, as you really have no idea how this is going to go. You should love the new you as you really want this new future. If you do not enjoy the new way then maybe you do not really want people to think of you in this way.

However, just doing and being the new way may not be enough, I am afraid. Be prepared for stubbornness and for blindness. You might need to speak explicitly and confess your changed version in full, e.g., "*You were right, I really needed to listen to you all more carefully.*" You may need to give a reason for such changes to have happened, e.g. "*I had my 360 and really saw that I needed to be more authoritative,*" or, "*After my experience at the food bank I realised I should show more compassion.*" Consider what others might gain from changing their minds. Can they be more confident now? Or perhaps they can give you more responsibility? If there is nothing in it for them, why on earth would they notice and upgrade their assessments? It is your job to be sure you have changed and that they like this.

STRATEGY 9
Be really different

This strategy is a level further along the continuum that has "You right now" at one end and "You as others want you" at the other. Just be different. Right now.

You might say that it cannot be that easy - you cannot simply be different just because someone else wants you to be. For a moment, just pretend that you can. Just imagine that literally anything were possible and be clear that you can be anything anyone wants you to be, and that you get to choose what you do and how you do it. Then look at what a total transformation might look like. Does it mean you will take some particular action? Do you resign and take a new job? Do you take a stand for a particular issue? Do you put some money into something? Do you sell something? Do you look at relocating? Do you go for a new style? It could be that one simple act will do the job. However, it may not be quite so easy. If that is the case, then the next thing is to consider that your issue is a "being" issue. The good news about "being" is that you can shift this if you want to. You can "be" resigned and cynical about something or you can "be" playful about the exact same thing. This will have you turn your depressed acceptance of things being bad into a sense of humour that will leave you laughing about how ridiculous you are. You may wonder how you do this, so here is the golden formula.

The first step in this process is to get really clear and honest about how you are "being" or "relating" to this specific situation or issue. Make a list. You can see how you are being through answering the following questions:

> *What does this make me feel?*
> *What am I doing about this at the moment?*
> *When I think about this, what do I feel?*
> *What results do I have in this area at the moment?*
> *What is my experience in this area?*

You will soon get to see if you are being depressed and resigned, free and easy, determined and hard-working or alternatively, committed and energetic. No doubt you will only be considering it as a problem if it is not working for you, so the likelihood is that your "being" is a little on the negative or disempowering side.

The next thing to consider is that the way you are has an impact on you and on others. Take the time to really think about this. It is not easy or nice to do this as usually there are negative consequences of any perceived issue. It is seeing and feeling this impact that will allow you to see that there may be another way, however. Once you can see that others are brought down too, you can perhaps see the benefits in shifting perspective. Look at the positive consequences from these effects as there will be something keeping you in place. Look at what it would take for you to drop these issues and to pick up another and different way of relating to this issue. It may be as easy as letting go of a pen... try it.

Choosing a new approach takes work. If you are not practised at this, you may need some support or coaching. The access to it is a belief that you can indeed choose how you relate to something. Tips for access are asking yourself the following questions:

> *What do I really want?*
> *What am I really getting out of my current approach?*
> *What am I losing with my current approach?*
> *What other costs are there?*
> *What could I add that would make a difference?*

Once you have a new and more empowering way of relating to your issue it will forever feel different, but this may not automatically turn into new action or a new way for any sustained length of time. This is because you may simply forget and return to a previous position. We are definitely creatures of habit! It may also be because other people do not necessarily notice the new you or allow you the space to behave differently. It is going to be up to you to sustain and remind; to keep in action and to maintain the new you. What can be helpful is to get really clear what you will do in the future, in terms of a positive action. This requires you to answer the following statement:

Next time I find myself doing:

....

then I will say/do:

....

RESOLUTION

A senior manager in a large regulatory body was exhausted and stressed. His 360 data was impressive, with some areas with hints of "could try harder". He was an expert in his specialism and he was now managing a big team, too. Through the feedback session he got clear that he had been trying to do a good job in all areas with the result that many parties were asking more and more of him. It had become totally unmanageable. He saw that he was trying to please and impress everyone and that the idea of disappointing someone important felt impossible. He was losing control and sleep, but he really wanted to make a big difference to his public through his work. The costs on him and his family were enormous and the risk was that the public was going to lose out on the best deal. What he saw that he could add that would make a difference was peace and calm, combined with confident assertiveness. Standing in this "being" allowed him to see that he could prioritise and share with key parties powerfully. He shifted from being a casualty to others' requests to being a leader of his own destiny.

To help him keep to his new position he confirmed that:
"Next time I find myself feeling pressured by too many requests, I will say that I will consider them, take some time and clarify my priorities."

This is a simple but profound strategy - get committed and be different, whichever way works for you.

CHAPTER 9

Strategies to change opinions

PART 3 - Change your context

STRATEGY 10
Give them a reason why you might change

If you want people to change their mind you need to make it easy for them. The easiest route is to make a visible and significant change yourself that will mean you will indeed be different. There are three areas of change you can influence in this regard:

1. Change your circumstances

Take on a new job, new responsibilities, have new support or a new boss, take on a new project, have a new big experience. To fulfil the requirements it has to be big enough a change for everyone to expect you to be different. Literally anyone would indeed change in these new circumstances. Not all circumstances can be managed by you at your will so look out for opportunities that simply present themselves and take them wholeheartedly. As an example, an ambitious sales executive in a large electronics company was looking to prove he was worthy of promotion. He took on contributing to a corporate initiative driving customer service. This took him way out of his comfort zone as he had not been known or seen as a people leader or customer champion and this initiative proved he was both. He made a difference to the company and changed his reputation. This project ran for only a year but it had a profound impact on his career, with a promotion soon showing up.

2. Learn from a big insight

Use feedback or a learning experience to the full and leverage the opportunity it provides to give others a really good reason why you might change. 360° feedback is a great way to do this because it involves so many people and it can be quite visible as a process. To reap the benefits of this, however, you have to be brave enough to talk about it and make the connection evident and undisputable to others around you. Share what you have learnt without malice or upset and tell people how you have changed, about how you are aiming to do things differently. Check with them what they have seen and ask for their help. This vulnerability and openness will encourage people to see your honest and authentic efforts. 360 is dramatic enough to lead someone to change, so use it to do just that.

3. Try a new intention

Get clear what your intention and desire had been and reinvent your future. Look hard at whether that intention had worked for you and for them and rethink what you are truly committed to. You can commit to something different. This is the time to stop focusing on your usual motives, e.g. impressing others, being a great boss, being useful, doing a good job and updating them, to something that inspires you afresh. Consider intentions of learning and growth rather than focusing on results, of delivering your purpose, of making a difference, of empowering other people, for instance. Alternatively you might want to consider getting yourself out of the way! The point is that your intentions can be altered and it will make the world of difference to what you do and how you do it. You and your relationships will likely start to shift immediately. An example of this was a senior arts academic who had recently joined a well-established (possibly traditional) university and had completed a 360° feedback. His strengths were obvious and clear. He was creative, imaginative, engaging and totally inspirational, but most of his reviewers thought he was lacking a sense of reality. They did not quite believe in him. This was seriously holding him back in his ability to deliver results through others. This perspective was a shock, but when he got clear that his intention had been to be "himself" and "show this old-fashioned place how to do things", he could see that he had been too much for this particular culture and these people. He decided to take on another intention, which was to empower and enable the team to move forward. The result was that he relaxed and became more measured in his approach. He listened more carefully and obviously, and he switched from being keen to present his own ideas to being more interested in other people's. Two years later he was promoted to head of his college and highly respected in this role.

In this type of situation it helps to clarify explicitly that you have changed. People may not yet have seen or noticed it, so it is important that you signpost it; people can be surprisingly easy to influence if you tell them what to think (as long as it is backed up with the significant reason, of course). Tell them and tell them again. Check with them that it is sustained. People can forget so you want to be sure to enforce the point over time.

STRATEGY 11
Start afresh

You might decide that you want to be different and better and you want to be known differently from how you are now and that starting again in a totally fresh environment might be the best option for you. There are two main circumstances which fit this approach - a fractured relationship with an individual or a community, and where you decide you would prefer to be within a different culture.

This strategy is an obvious one when a 360° feedback has shown you that a relationship is broken and/or where there has been a betrayal. You can spot "broken" relationships when the data is showing up with strongly negative ratings and/or harsh comments. A clearly broken relationship can be seen when even the higher ratings are tempered by barbed comments. A 360 comment I saw the other day was from a direct report who had given a large proportion of "1" and "2" ratings (defined as "poor" and "fair" on a 5-point rating scale). There were some "5"s against behaviours such as "Shows drive and determination", but comments against this question included, "Too tough with own team", and "Should listen to others more". Specific questions to look at for broken relationships are those connected to trust, honesty and fairness, as well as delivery of promises and commitments. Poor ratings in these areas smack of a perceived lack of integrity and can imply the foundation of relationship has been shaken. As mentioned earlier, if you identify these specifics you can, of course, look at what you can do to fix these things, but at the end of the day they may be pretty unfixable. Whatever you do, the other party may not be willing to forgive and forget. They may be unwilling to let go of their views even though there may be a pretence that things are OK. You can attempt to get things complete but in the end you may need to accept the relationship the way it is. Whether you want to continue working with this relationship affecting you and others around you is up to you. Starting afresh will usually be very much easier and definitely less stressful for you - definitely worth looking at as an option.

Betrayal is the key act that has a fresh start be a real option - whether you have been seen to betray someone or someone else has considered you as having betrayed them or whether you have been betrayed yourself. Betrayal puts a chasm between two people where only a bridge can be built. The ground between you will never be quite the same again. What is important is that you know you have a choice in the matter. You can work alongside this broken relationship, as you already no doubt have been. Or you can confront it head on with a fresh intention or insight. Or you can walk away to pastures new with the full learning and experience that this experience has provided. You will be able to turn a corner into a new field and a fresh context with a stronger sense of yourself, knowing that even a broken relationship can be managed and survived.

To move forward in a new and strong position, you need to get clear as to what has happened in the past and to commit and repromise. It is a conversation of sharing, of confessing, and then it is one of declaring and making new agreements.

The other situation that calls for a fresh start is when you decide you want to be in a different environment or culture. You may see yourself as "counter-cultural" currently, i.e., your style rubs up against some key values in the pervading environment. You may feel "pigeonholed" as a result of how you contrast with others around you. You may be deeply unmotivated and uninspired by those around you. You may feel it is simply a good time for a change of scene. All of these reasons may lead you to consider creating a new future for yourself in a different sector or culture. Such brave moves may be scary, but are often looked back on with the knowledge and certainty that they were the most transformational and developmental actions of your life. If this strategy is calling you, be bold and consider moving on.

CHAPTER 10

Embrace your personal stereotype

You do not really want to mind what other people think about you. Why should you? Yet at the same time, as we have seen, what other people think does indeed affect you every minute of every day in subtle and less subtle ways. These circular positions persist over time, for much longer than seems to be necessary (although perhaps our viewpoint on stereotypes tends to be rather short-term, if you consider the age of humanity). The strategies described here are likely to bring consciousness to your own biases of others and those impacting you, too. As such, it then becomes critical for you to be OK with this, otherwise you can end up feeling depressed and resigned about your lot in the stereotype game. This is a game that is much older and bigger than you, or even your generation.

First, it is helpful to really know yourself well and to understand how you come across from every angle that is important to you. It makes sense, but it is not so easy. How can you possibly understand yourself fully from everyone else's angle when you only have your own angle to look from? It may be an impossible task, but it is still worth attempting to do and worth taking this on as a lifelong exploration and curiosity. Self-awareness can now be proved to help productivity and performance [26] and is acknowledged as a key and critical part of having a growth mindset[27], but really looking at yourself takes something. Self-insight is not just linked to a learning mindset. **Howard Gardner** in *"Extraordinary Minds"* (1997) concluded that exceptional individuals have *"a special talent for identifying their own strengths and weaknesses"*. You need a little courage and an openness to hear what others have to say, even when you know (or fear) that you may not like it.

Being offered "feedback", however, has been seen to cause significant anxiety in neurological experiments. Functional MRI scans can show reactions to such a prospect akin to when you are walking in a dark alley and hear footsteps approach behind you… so this is not to be considered lightly. Our very safety and the very preciousness of our self-identity is at stake. But just imagine being brave in that alley, stopping your walk and instead standing firm and turning to see what horrors are behind you. You are likely to find a human being, as logical and illogical as you, with views formed from generations of culture and inherited values and judgements combined with a lifetime of reinforcing experience. That's all! So be brave and turn around. Take a look, ask, interview, gather detailed feedback using a 360° feedback process[28], generally enquire and check. Closed questions work a dream if you think people will hesitate to really say - make it easy for them to give you the news. Ask the question you dread, e.g., "*I'm really quite mean/lazy/reckless/hasty/difficult, aren't I?*" You may be surprised at the outcome.

Just a quick word about surprising feedback. Learning something new about yourself can leave you feeling upset, angry, emotional and a bunch of other negative responses. It is worth understanding how this process works so you are prepared for what might happen. Consider new information about you as being processed just like bad news. Hearing the bad results of a medical test from a doctor can lead to a similar reaction. The grieving process was described earlier. How to feel better? Well, first you need to work through what it means, why it has happened and see what your role was in the whole process. Once you can take full responsibility for it you can start to reach a position of acceptance and you will ultimately end up integrating the new ideas re your self-identity to form an updated, more mature self-identity. I still remember clearly getting some feedback from a twenty-two-year-old guy who happened to be on a personal development course with me. We were having fun. I was thirty-nine or so and, from my perspective, in the prime of life, but obviously more mature than him. There was an exercise we had to do and as a result we had to describe each other. He described me as "middle-aged" and I saw in those two words a whole heap of meaning - a lack of respect, a sense of being different from him, an assumption that I was "past it" and in the same category as his mother rather than a peer. A number of slightly puzzling things he had said earlier in the day suddenly made more sense. I got it. Nothing was wrong. When I was twenty-two I expect I thought thirty-nine-year old women were middle-aged and not like me. What's the big deal? I was upset, though! My identity did not include middle-age! I realised I did not like being treated with disrespect. It took me a while to process this and get OK, but knowing and accepting his position meant the relationship flowed better; it was somehow based on more truth than before. What I then started to notice was that he had a huge respect for me as, to him, I was supremely inspiring given what I was doing at my "age"! I had not noticed this before. The truth may hurt you in the short term, but in the long term it will help.

Apart from seeking feedback, it's also useful to look closely at the facts that have made you this way so far. This is your truth. You were born the day and the time and place you were born, to your mother and your father (and/or others). You were born to a certain family with particular values in a particular culture and environment. You had money or you did not. You had siblings or you were alone. You may have been born in a religious environment, you may have moved house, you may have been brought up with a certain accent, with particular expectations, and friends that helped or hindered you. You have had particular health and energy, with corresponding ambition and determination. You have had active support and sponsors or you have had no assistance. You have had personality traits and strengths. You have a particular style some other people did not like so much. You have had a particular physique and gender. You had braces as a teenager or you did not. You then put in effort (or not) and had successes and failures. You applied for places or jobs and you got them or you did not. You then saw them through or you did not. You fell in love or you did not and your relationships went a certain way. You had children or you did not. Masses of facts are relevant to who you are now. If you look at them hard you will notice that many of them you cannot change now. Some of them you have never been able to change, actually.

You are the way you are because of all these facts. They uniquely make you, no one else. You may as well love it!

If you list these facts and look at how they all fit together you will see the logic of it all. Stand away from yourself a little and look from afar. A sensitive girl born in a northern city in the UK in 1962 to intelligent, ambitious working-class parents, who moved south to a prosperous suburb of London where she is very tall and skinny and speaks "funny", is set up a certain way. All the other pieces in the story make sense. She is energetic and driven, but not physically strong. Not surprising that three children and a busy business later there might be well-being challenges! Look how perfectly it all fits together. Even the upsets, the breakdowns, the disappointments and the failures. They all make sense. This is you and your life and it is how you are running it. You are the author of your story and you will make sure that the storyline makes sense. That is your job.

You may be happy with everything in your story and everything about you that other people think. Brilliant. Most of us, however, face the reality of not being happy with everything about ourselves. Of not easily accepting some factors we cannot change. This failure of acceptance may be a phenomenon of the current age where we expect to "have it all". Things have changed in a few of the major stereotypes. Gender is an example. Expectations have changed significantly through each of the last five generations, at least. A girl born today in the UK will likely have an expectation of a career and family of her choosing, and of the vote and of economic independence. Inside this context of freedom it is harder to accept limitations imposed upon us.

Look at relishing all your facts, look at the good points and really appreciate them. Focus on feeling gratitude and thank the people around you for their role in the matter. Look at appreciating the facts you do not like that much, too. Look hard at the good side of these facts. Know and believe that every fact has a good side and a bad side. For a while, when I was not well enough to properly run and manage my business and it was causing me considerable stress, I decided that having a business was a bad thing and that I should sell it or give it over to someone else. Other people told me I should do that, too. In the end a friend offered to help me manage it and I managed to get myself back into being well enough and positive enough to consider my business as my asset and my blessing. How else could I make such a difference in the corporate world, leveraging my specialist skills with a workload and travel challenge that could fit my extrovert energy, as well as the school runs!? Turning my relationship to this fact from one of resistance and blame to one of gratitude and thankfulness made the difference.

A technique to help you relish your personal facts and to bring to light your true personal brand is one of exaggeration. Write down your characteristics in the table below and then make them ten times bigger/worse/stronger - write down what they look like now:

My personal facts	My exaggerated facts
For example:	*For example:*
Tall and slender	*Supermodel slim and elegant*
55 years old, mother of three	*Elegant, wise witch and matriarch*
Owns and runs own business	*Super rich and successful entrepreneur*

Your personal facts	Your exaggerated facts

Does that help you love who you are? If you still need help to do this, then do seek support and input from a buddy or expert coach/ counsellor. It is really worth getting to a strong position.

Now you can really create the brand you want for yourself - one that is based on the truth and the facts about you and one that you can really relish and expand. Write down all these tricky-to-change factors and include everything else that you love, too. Include your quirky characteristics. The things people see in you and the things you know about yourself.

The personal brand I want for myself is:

For example:

Inspiring and feminine mother. A super-sensitive people-person, who enjoys the excitement of working with and contributing to people in a context of growth, sharing her ideas and tools so others have access to satisfaction and development.

The personal brand you want for yourself is:

Check that you love everything you write down and that it is all totally true. Again, get expert input if you need assistance. Once you have written this down, revisit it later to see if you can increase the inspiration and desirable qualities within it and to take out any untruths. Work on it and then treasure it. Capture it somewhere really useful, such as your phone or your computer. Translate it into a collage or a visual representation that you can put up in your bedroom for daily reference. Check that it inspires you, calls you and makes you feel grateful and positive. If it does not do all these things then refine it further so that it does. This is your story and your future and you can influence it your way[29].

Once you have your brand, you can be the author of your final chapters. You can plan, you can see what happens, you can have a well-considered strategy. You get to be the type of author you want to be. What will serve you best right now is to trust and believe that your future is fine, whatever is in it. You get a choice about how you approach and manage the opinions of others inside of this. You do not get a choice about certain things, but you do have freedom to accept and be powerful in this area. You get to laugh, question, explore, exaggerate and enjoy others' biases that you see work against and for you. You can be upset or resigned about them and, of course, you can be totally unconscious if you would rather. My suggestion is to have a go at playing with them first, though.

Concluding remarks

Opinions are rife and their spread these days can be fast and even viral. But they are not fatal and they are not directly life-limiting. They may be opportunity-limiting, though. Others' opinions will encourage and discourage you, empower and disempower. Even a neutrality can provide a negative energetic influence in the expectation and hope of support.

There are forces at play affecting us more than we know. They are not easy to control or manage, but they are there. Given that, it would be easy to feel helpless in these matters, but with these eleven strategies, alternatives are available. There is a chance through expanding general consciousness about such matters that we can upgrade our stereotypic thinking to being a little more about real observations combined with a big dose of possibility, rather than pure prejudice.

References

[1] D. Rock, "SCARF: A Brain-Based Model for Collaborating With and Influencing Others", *NeuroLeadership Journal*, 1, 44-52 (2008)

[2] Elva R. Ainsworth, "*360 Degree Feedback: A Transformational Approach*, (2016)"

[3] D. Rooke and W. Torbert, "Seven Transformations of Leadership", *Harvard Business Review*, (April 2005)

[4] P. Rozin and E. B. Royzman, "Negativity Bias, Negativity Dominance, and Contagion" *Personality and Social Psychology Review*, Vol. 5, No. 4, 296-320, (2001)

R. F. Baumeister et al, "Bad is Stronger Than Good", *Review of General Psychology* 5(4), 323-370, published by Educational Publishing Foundation, (Dec 2001)

[5] "R. Hanson, "The Neuroscience of Happiness", *Greater Good Magazine*, (23 Sep 2010)

[6] See the paper on "Gender and 360°" available on www.talentinnovations.com and "How Gender Bias Corrupts Performance Reviews, and What to Do About It", Dr Paola Cecchi-Dimeglio, Harvard Law School - *Harvard Business Review*, (2017): https://hbr.org/2017/04/how-gender-bias-corrupts-performance-reviews-and-what-to-do-about-it

[7] *Psychological Science*, Vol 19 #3, (2008)

[8] Invented in 1955 by Joseph Luft and Harrington Ingham, this is an information processing tool for the purpose of self-awareness, personal and group development and strengthening trusting relationships

[9] Cornell University's School of Industrial and Labor Relations in partnership with Green Peak Partners International Consulting, "*When It Comes to Business Leadership, Nice Guys Finish First*", (2010)

[10] B. Wansink & J. Sobal, *Journal of Environment and Behaviour*, Vol: 39 issue: 1, page(s): 106-123, 2007

[11] Published in the journal "*Attention, Perception, and Psychophysics*"

[12] K. Cameron, C. Mora, T. Leutscher & M. Calarco, "Effects of Positive Practices on Organisational Effectiveness", *Journal of Applied Behavioural Science*, Vol 47, Issue 3, (2011)

[13] https: //implicit.harvard. edu/implicit/takeatest.html

[14] G. A. Kelly, *Theory of Personality: The Psychology of Personal Constructs*, New York: Norton (1955)

[15] See the paper on "Competency frameworks" available on www.talentinnovations.com

[16] Oxford Dictionary

17 Oxford Dictionary

18 See the "Gender and 360°" paper on www.talentinnovations.com

19 See Eckhart's interesting videos: https://www.eckharttolle.com/

20 Professor P. Ekman, *Emotions Revealed,* (2004)

21 Definition from Oxford Living Dictionary

22 See www.elvaainsworth.co.uk

23 Oxford Dictionary

24 Seen in *Huffington Post,* (3 October 2017)

25 Cambridge Dictionary

26 Cornell's University School of Industrial and Labor Relations, (2010)

27 Dr C. Dweck, *"Mindset,"* (2017)

28 See website www.talentinnovations.com for a free trial

29 Rhonda Byrne, *"The Secret,"* (2007)

Made in the USA
Lexington, KY
16 May 2018